MOVE TO PROFIT

A CEO's Guide to Relocating Your Business, Navigating Risk and Increasing Your Bottom Line

Stacia Hobson

Move To Profit

*A CEO's Guide to Relocating Your Business,
Navigating Risk and Increasing Your Bottom Line*

Stacia Hobson

Copyright © 2023
All Rights Reserved.

Published by Stacia Hobson

No part of this publication may be reproduced, distributed, or transmitted in any form or by any means, including photocopying, recording, or other electronic or mechanical methods, without the prior written permission of the publisher, except in the case of brief quotations embodied in critical reviews and certain other noncommercial uses permitted by copyright law.

Disclaimer: The author makes no guarantees concerning the level of success you may experience by following the advice and strategies contained in this book, and you accept the risk that results will differ for each individual and corporation. The purpose of this book is to educate, motivate and inspire.

For more information: support@staciahobson.com
ISBN: 979-8-9893046-0-8 (print)
ISBN: 979-8-9893046-1-5 (e-book)

To show my appreciation for your investment in my book, here's a bonus gift to help you clarify, investigate and take action.

Some of the free resources in this book include:

- Mindset Strategy - How to overcome all the objections in order to look at life options that are available to you.
- A Site Selection guide - Pertinent questions to ask.
- A Grant Checklist - Define what you absolutely need and what you want.
- Tips on how to successfully vet the workforce
- A checklist on managing your current workforce
- Tips on how to successfully recruit a new workforce
- Training Checklist - what you thought you knew but didn't

Get your free gifts here:
www.staciahobson.com

Table of Contents

Chapter 1: Is a Move Right for you?.. 11
Chapter 2: How to Leverage Economic Grants 19
Chapter 3: Other Considerations for Negotiating and Site Selection 27
Chapter 4: How to Vet the Workforce.. 37
Chapter 5: Can the Community Step Up to the Training Needs 45
Chapter 6: How to Manage the Existing Workforce 53
Chapter 7 : Rebuilding your Workforce... 63
Chapter 8: How to Hire/Recruit a New Workforce............................... 71
Chapter 9: How to Train a New Workforce 83
Chapter 10: Pace and Logistics of the Move... 87
Chapter 11: Aftermath... 95
Chapter 12.. 101
Acknowledgments... 107
About the Author... 109

"Opportunity is missed by most people because it is dressed in overalls and looks like work."

—Thomas A Edison

Chapter 1
Is a Move Right for you?

Is it reckless? Maybe. But what do dreams know of boundaries?
—Amelia Earhart

Mindset

My story begins back in 2017 with grant money. I was in a tiff about the fact that I was a small-to-medium-sized employer, and I struggled in getting grant money. Contrary to common belief, it is the small-to-medium-sized employers who are the backbone of this country, not the Caterpillars, John Deere's etc. The mom-and-pop shops employ more than the big fish and in my opinion offer greater job stability because they are invested in the workforce.

I was invited to a NAWBO, National Association of Women Business Owners, and sitting at my table was this lovely woman named Jen. She and I started chatting, and I realized she was a consultant who helped companies like mine get grants or tax advantages. She point blank asked me if I would be willing to move. I said yes.

By saying yes, I automatically opened up a whole other realm of possibilities. You see, the thing about having an open mind is that when you say yes, even without action, flood gates open.

My business partner, who is my brother, and I had discussed the horrible financial & policy conditions of Illinois for years. The tax situation in Illinois for property and income is unreal. We were paying $100K in property taxes on my property, my brother's, and the plant. That was after we approached the tax assessors for a reduction due to the 2008 crash. Then we were paying another $100K in income taxes.

Granted, I am thrilled to be so blessed to have to pay those taxes, but I was like *Illinois, get control of your budget.* Illinois policy makers could not, would not get a balanced budget, nor are they likely to ever create a balanced budget.

About a month after meeting Jen in May of 2017, the Illinois General Assembly passed a 32 percent income tax hike and a 33 percent corporate tax hike. This was the largest permanent income tax hike in Illinois history. Translated, our personal income tax increased to 4.95 percent from 3.75 percent, and the corporate income tax increased to 7 percent from 5.25 percent. It was a double whammy, and literally the next day on May 24, 2017, Blake received an email from another site selection consulting group, The Next Move, about relocating our business.

Since I was the one all about government grants, I spearheaded this project. I went to their webinar and had them in for a face-to-face meeting within a few weeks. Our main competitors are in Ohio, a very friendly business state, which left us at a pretty tough disadvantage.

Believe it or not, our customers really don't care about the unfair taxing policies of Illinois, but maybe yours do. They really don't care if my cost of doing business is higher—they are not going to pay a few cents more for their widgets versus my competition.

Chapter 1

While we took on the site selection investigation, Illinois' Governor Pritzker passed an additional 7.9 percent personal income tax hike that also included businesses. Gas tax went from .19 per gallon to .38 per gallon. They also passed a gradual minimum-wage increase to grow from $10 an hour to $15 an hour by 2025. We pay all of our team members above minimum wage, but this law forces an upwards sliding scale.

At the end of the day, in order to create the desire to uproot your world, your *why* has to be pretty big, as does your vision. We were so done with Illinois robbing us due to poor policy and policy being made by folks who never, not one day of their lives, were responsible for a profit and loss statement. Further, with Illinois being the third most moved out of state, the taxing situation will not improve—at least not in the near future.

Considering uprooting your business or opening a new branch in another part of the country is not for the faint of heart. It is a risky proposition, but the upside can be most profitable and rewarding. I have done three company moves, and all have proven to be the right choice for us.

Before we go any further, you need to make a decision. This does not mean committing to anything other than an open mindset. When you say *yes* to what life brings to your doorstep, amazing things happen.

When I announced our move, I cannot count how many people told me why they could not move. It was interesting to me that they could not comprehend the move and what it meant, as they were stuck in partial shock. But mostly, they thought this option was meant for other people, not them.

Reasons included but were not limited to: "I have a customer who likes to stop by the shop every week." "I cannot leave my family." "This is a family business." "My workforce is too valuable." "I will lose my customers."

I am not negating any of these reasons—or really, excuses. They are all valid concerns that may or may not need to be addressed. However, I am here to tell you that they all can be managed or resolved. It is interesting to me that none of these really occurred to me. I never once thought it was not possible, but I am a risk taker through and through.

I will guide you on how to manage those questions that keep you blocked from even exploring this opportunity. What other opportunities are you potentially missing out on because you have a closed mindset that does not allow you to see what could be?

Trust me, when I looked at moving—when it came right down to it—the answer was no. I did not want to move. But the prospective thrill of victory was overwhelming, even intoxicating. I knew I could do it, and instead of talking about how I hated Illinois and all the policies and taxes, I decided to something about it.

It is always far easier to complain about our circumstances than to take action. This is human nature. However, how many times have you advised your managers and team leads to not complain unless they also come to the table with a solution?

Why consider a move?

There are many reasons why people would consider a move. We think about them regularly. For example, I would love to live in that neighborhood. I just love that house. I would love to live in the

Hamptons. I would love to live in Tennessee. I wish I had a larger facility, or I need a larger facility. The daydreams go on. The reason why we change is because we think something better is out there. Something we don't have here is there—wherever there might be.

What would you consider? Where would you like to live? Why not make that "retirement" plan a "now" plan? Honestly, we did not think that Memphis was the retirement plan, but today we both love Memphis. Yes, I know it has all sorts of negative connotations. It is like all cities. Some areas are beautiful and others are not. Memphis is a small big town. Lots of great restaurants and shopping but without all the traffic. Their idea of bad traffic is a fifteen to twenty minute jam, and you are still traveling around thirty-five miles per hour. You cannot say that about Chicago, Atlanta, Los Angeles, or New York.

You must consider your biggest needs—whether it be personal or professional. My need was financial and to be in a business-friendly state. I wanted grant money to move and to train our team members, a better tax situation and a building that we could grow into. Our previous building was 67,500 square feet, and when we moved in, it was humongous. We were used to 35,000 square feet and never thought we would fill it up. Fifteen years later, we were busting at the seams of the 67,500 square feet facility.

Another consideration is your quality of life. What is your current quality of life? What would you like it to be in both the short and long term? I knew my short-term quality of life would suffer when we ultimately decided on Clarksdale. But I also thought that my long-term quality of life would be improved. If the business was in a better financial position and we were able to either pocket money saved versus paying more in taxes—or expanding the business versus paying more in taxes—then my exit strategy improved.

A huge consideration is labor. Are you meeting your current labor goals? Do you need labor? If you are a manufacturer in today's world, you probably need labor unless you are plateauing. Nothing wrong with coasting, as it allows you space to make improvements that are near impossible to make when you are growing. Very different space. Depending upon the location you choose, unskilled labor could be readily available. Even though the "available" labor force in my location is small, it is viable. Once I figured out the key to successfully hiring in this location, I ceased having labor availability issues.

Another huge bonus of moving to a business-friendly state is insurance and not just property and liability insurance—but workmen's compensation. My workmen's compensation insurance went from $80,000 to $20,000—equivalent to a mid-level manager's salary.

If you are at the point of starting to consider that this might be a possibility, not a decision, there are a few things you need to do now before you go any further. And actually, even if you don't think this is a possibility, these are a few things that you ought to review regardless. If you do not have any process templates in place, start getting that in order. If you have processes in place, begin reviewing them. I 100 percent guarantee you that there is still tribal knowledge not captured.

I thought we had solid—I mean solid—processes. Our new trainees were in training for only two weeks before they were let loose. I thought we were rock stars. *No. We sucked.* Trust me when I tell you: most likely, your processes are not full proof. Bring in someone or even yourself and see if you can run the job with no help based on the work instructions at hand. As owners, we get very removed from this detail, even though we may even oversee process generation.

The other item that you need to get on is creating inventory. If you are doing a close distance move—i.e. within an hour's drive from your current location—and the majority of your labor is coming to the new location, I would suggest building a minimum of two weeks ahead, at least initially. One month would be better.

If you are doing a long distance move and 30 percent or less of your labor is coming with you, then I would suggest building ahead a minimum of six to nine months, if you know how to recruit, retain and train a workforce from scratch.

I built ahead two months, thinking that with my labor training plan, it would be enough. It was not even close. In my case, twelve months would have been incredibly beneficial.

Chapter 2
How to Leverage Economic Grants

Everything is negotiable. Whether or not the negotiation is easy is another thing.

—Carrie Fisher

Site Selection Consultants

Much of this chapter is about mindset and where your thoughts are focused in relation to grant money. What you think you could have, should have, and deserve. I know that is a bold statement, but it is the truth.

My mindset from the start was that I 100 percent deserved to get rewarded for burdening all the risks that come with business ownership. Bold again, but I truly felt that Illinois was robbing me, and being a business that supported forty-six families, I deserved more in my pocket as compared to the government, which had yet to provide a balanced budget.

Regardless of your move distance, I would definitely recommend hiring a site selection consultant, unless you are moving *within* an unfriendly business state. Doing a lateral move will not reap grant benefits.

Ironically, if you are looking at moving into Illinois, you can get some nice grants. I would think that would be the same for any unfriendly business state. Illinois state or local counties and communities won't pay to keep you. They cannot afford to give up any cash reserves, and that is if they have them.

Consultants deal with economic development partners all the time. Every county has an economic development arm. Consultants know the grants that are available. They know the counties, as they have likely worked with them previously. Negotiating grant and move agreements is no different than negotiating pricing on any project or part, depending on your industry.

Nobody wants to leave money on the table. If the economic development doesn't have to give you the money, then they won't. Just like if I don't have to lower my price on my widget, I won't. Site selection consultants know or can find out what the state and counties have to offer as well as what they are willing to offer. Just like in your business, you more than likely know what your competitors are able and not able to do.

How to find a site selection consultant? I already had an open mindset around this topic, which was extremely beneficial. I was looking for grant money, so my thoughts were all about "grant money." You know how, when you want to buy a new vehicle, you then see that vehicle all the time? That is because your focus lies on that vehicle. Your brain seeks what it is told to find.

I met one person who had just started her business as a move consultant, and then a few months later, I met the site selection consultant, The Next Move Group, we signed with. I did not do any looking. They found us because I was already open to having that come my way.

We hired the consultants because they felt right to me. If you are not actively looking for grants, you can find site selection consultants via an internet search. They are on LinkedIn, but not very active, which makes finding them a little more difficult on that particular platform.

How do you vet a site selection consultant? One: do they know their stuff? Let them tell you what they can do for you. How many moves have they previously done? What is their depth of knowledge? This is key. Talk to them and determine if they are knowledgeable and can negotiate on your behalf and theirs.

Typically they work on commission. They will charge an upfront fee, which I asked to be reimbursed if we did move. Their real payment comes from a percentage of what they negotiate for you. Of course, get professional references. Make sure you like and trust them. This is not a quick process. It took us two years of looking and contemplating before we signed. You will be spending a lot of time with your consultant—more than you think. There is travel time, be it in a car or in the air. There will be many dinners together, many calls, and many meetings. If you don't like them, don't sign up with them, as they are truly your business partner until the papers are signed.

Request For Proposal (RFP)

Your first meeting with your consultant will develop the outline for the request for proposal, which will be submitted to the communities. You need to determine your must haves, your would be nice to have, and your wants. This will become clearer as you move through the process. My advice here is to ask for everything. This is not the time to be conservative or bashful. If you want to be in a community that offers you a lake lifestyle nearby, then ask for it. If you want a manufacturing facility, then ask for it.

Consider the money it will cost you to move. This was a big number for us, as we are cold headers and our equipment is big. We estimated the cost to move our equipment was $700,000. This did not include the cost to move all the miscellaneous lathes, mills, grinding equipment, tools, etc. This is not a small cost. We had a 67,500-square-foot facility, and it took us thirty truckloads to move. We did not consider this in our initial move dollars. This added another $100,000. Be as upfront as possible with the must haves. Our must haves include a large enough building with 480 power. Money to move the equipment. Viable work force and of course training money. Our needs were things like freight accessibility and secondary outside operations. Our wants were things like community and extracurricular activities.

You also need to decide what states you would consider moving to. We chose twelve states simply because of their friendly tax structure—or at least friendlier than Illinois'. We needed to be in a business-friendly state so that we could be more competitive. Let's face it: we make steel fasteners, and both our largest competitors are in Ohio. Ohio is a business-friendly state, and as a result, their costs to produce are substantially lower than ours simply due to taxes.

Since we moved, Illinois has passed other laws, forcing labor costs to go up across the board through minimum-wage mandates, and most recently, paid time-off mandates. It is just so irritating to have the government meddle in your business. Our list was Kentucky, Texas, Tennessee, Wisconsin, Indiana, Missouri, Minnesota, Arkansas, New Mexico, Ohio, Georgia, and North Carolina. Notice, Mississippi was not on the list.

Your consultants will send out the request for proposals to these states. The states will review the request and send it out to the communities that might be interested. They will put in a closing date, and then you wait to see what communities respond. Once the proposals are returned, you will review them with your consultant.

We had 169 proposals, which is astounding. Even our consultants were taken aback. How do you sort through so many? Further, each proposal return is what can be considered an initial offering. Every community that responds will submit an initial proposal of what they will do to entice you to move.

Our consultants took the lead. They had all the communities listed across the top of a spreadsheet, the offerings going vertically down, and a check box of what each community could provide. They basically eliminated communities in which they knew their initial offering was all that they had to offer and communities that they did not think would be a match. They recommended communities that they knew would improve their proposals as the process ensued.

Think of it like dating. The more that the communities get to know you, the more that they will reveal to you. We ended up looking at communities from Ohio, Texas, Tennessee, New Mexico, Arkansas, Missouri, Georgia and Kentucky. It was so disappointing that Indiana and Wisconsin really did not step up, as either of those would have been an easier move.

Interview the Communities

Next step is to interview those communities. There were thirty-three presentations over three days. Some folks were far more seasoned than others. Several were very funny from our perspective. We had "army" and "navy" from Butler MO. I think this was their first presentation ever. One lady had been in the army and the other in the navy. They played off that and were so disorganized but had a lot of passion. How can you resist passion, right?

The other one that was shocking was Clifford from Blytheville, Arkansas. Clifford was an older southern gentleman with a curled mustache, dressed in a suit with a vest and a bow tie. It worked. He got up, and his out-of-the-gate offer blew us away. His opener was, "We have a 40,000 square foot building that we will give you. We will add on 25,000 square feet at our expense." *Wow.* He goes on to say, "Let's just talk about the pink elephant in the room." What pink elephant? When did the pink elephant arrive? He said, "Yes, let's just talk about the blacks. The community is black. Many don't like 'em. Rest assured you can live in a community that has no blacks."

You could have pushed me over with a feather. I am from the north, and we don't talk about black people like this. I was shocked twice now by this unassuming gentleman, and I don't shock easily, as most who have employees don't.

After three days and thirty-three presentations, I was overwhelmed. We had to go through another elimination process. We decided to eliminate Ohio—they had six presentations. But they really didn't bring anything more to the plate from the initial proposal. We eliminated Tennessee because they lost the building. I was disappointed about that, as it was a brand new facility, and the plans looked amazing. Further, that town's economic development had just won another proposal for 200 jobs, so that might have caused a labor shortage.

Always have faith that things will work out for you. New Mexico was eliminated not because of their offer but because of its location. I really thought it would be a challenge for material movement, as most of our audience is in Illinois and in the south. We got down to ten locations as potential move sites.

How do you determine which communities stay on the list? My brother, being the engineer, decided that we needed the net present value of each community, and any community that was better than Huntley, Illinois would get site visits. Hugely inconvenient for our consulting group, but they did it, and seven of the ten scored higher. This left two communities in Arkansas; Lexington, Kentucky; Butler, Missouri; two communities in Georgia; and Longview, Texas.

Site Visits

Then the next phase began. We started scheduling site visits. My brother and I hardly did anything together, so when we went out of town for the first time, it caused a huge hubbub within the company. I am not sure why, but it created much disrest. We found out because we had an employee that was thinking about buying a house close to work, and we felt it was only right to trust this employee with our thoughts about potentially moving the company, as neither of us wanted his move to be closer to work be a short-term plan. From that point forward, we opted to take the day before or after off. My brother often "worked from home." We met at the airport instead of at the plant and advised our team of our whereabouts to keep people calm.

What you need to know is that the incentives get much richer at this point. Now is the time to really get clear on what you need financially to make this work. Every site visit must be thought of as a move. Keep in mind you still have not said yes to anything, other than an open mindset. Now is the time to really start vetting the labor, vetting the building, vetting the community, and vetting the training opportunities. What can the community do to support this event?

We loved Lexington from a personal perspective, but Lexington did not have a building, and while they could offer some training, I knew it would not be enough. Also on site visits, it is imperative that you speak to other business owners and HR management without the presence of the director of economic development. The existing businesses know the state of the community and want to help the community for sure, but they don't want to see you fail either. I found that they cannot give you the true story under watchful eyes, as they don't want to be the ones who ruin it for the community.

Chapter 3
Other Considerations for Negotiating and Site Selection

If you are not hearing the word "no" on occasion, then you are not asking for enough.

—Linda Swindling

What else should you be negotiating during these site visits?

Labor: the less desirable the community, the more labor dollars you will need for the lift. What do I mean by labor dollars? Training, training, training. Ask for funding to pay a trainer, even if it is one of your own team members to train. I highly recommend you pull trainers in from another company nearby, from the local workforce development college, or from another workforce development in another town, instead of having your own staff do extra training. Yes, the labor sector for economic development should be able to figure this piece out for and with you.

Ask for payroll tax credits if they have not yet already offered it up. Go for longevity. We have 4 percent for ten years as long as we keep our negotiated number at fifty people. Our 4 percent tax credits apply to those folks making a minimum of $27,500 annually, or at least $13.22 an hour. I pay well, so almost all my people count. However, I would negotiate that minimum annual income down as much as possible. This is some serious money. I have a two million dollar payroll; this equates to about $80,000 every year for ten years.

The obvious—coming from a high tax state—is property, both real and real estate tax abatement for an extended time. This is not the time to be bashful. Some states tax real property—i.e., what is in the facility, as well as real estate. This is common in the south. At any rate, we negotiated no taxes for fifteen years.

Negotiate for the building itself, regardless of whether it is existing or greenfield. All of this is negotiable. We had several locations literally give us a building. The place in Mississippi is a 142,000 square foot facility that we did not have to pay anything on for the first two years, and then our monthly expense is about $2500. Yes, you read that correctly: a *monthly* cost of $2,500. Then in ten years, we owe another $1,000, and then the building is ours. We were able to get $300,000 for building improvements, and we used every cent and then have put in our own money to deal with what was unknown.

If possible, do a deep dive on the mechanics, the electrical and the foundation of the building. Though this is a little tricky, and we were not successful because we didn't even think about it. We moved, and our equipment kept blowing out. Our plant manager, along with our on staff electrician, finally figured out that nothing was grounded. All you folks from highly regulated states, sit down—yes, this is the gospel truth. That was a $100,000 expense out of left field.

Above all, keep in mind that all communities, facilities, and greensites will all have their pros and cons. You and only you can determine what you can and cannot live with. Clarksdale is ninety minutes from Memphis. Both my brother and I have homes just outside of Memphis simply to get out of Clarksdale. We both love Memphis.

Seriously, four years ago I thought Memphis was seedy and nasty, which is what most northerners think. Just like any city, it has its good and not so good parts. But Memphis is a small—population of one million—big city. Good shopping and restaurants. Easy to get around. Parking and traffic are not an issue. They complain about their traffic, and really it is a fifteen minute delay, and you are typically still moving at forty miles per hour. Coming from Chicago— not even Atlanta or LA—this is nothing.

Keep in mind that the more desperate the community, the richer the offer. Blytheville, Arkansas is in a bad way, and that is why their offer was so rich. We are from a middle class community. When we moved to Huntley, it was a sleepy little farming town with economic development already in action. Within our first five years, the community had tripled in size to 30,000 people. Towns like Blytheville and Clarksdale, where the financial offers were massive, had both suffered a huge economic hit due to industry changing in both of those communities. In Blytheville's case, the air force base closed. In Clarksdale, the railroad industry changed. Both were devastating to the community, and neither had enough effort toward economic development until after the fact.

The site visits will make it pretty easy to make further cuts. We really liked Butler, Missouri. I really thought that we would be fine. Sadly, the two newbies blew the deal. They had a manufacturing facility that had been vacant for years and years. It had been up for sale at a very reasonable price. Our consultants told them to buy the building and then work a deal with us. The girl in charge could not wrap her head around this concept.

In retrospect, I should have called the other woman and been like, "Look, this is what has to happen in order for us to move forward with Butler." As a result, the owner got word that there might be interest in the facility and jacked up the price, making it unaffordable for Butler and for us, given that it needed a lot of work. At this point, you should cut your possible locations down to two to four to go back and revisit.

The revisit may be your deciding factor, or there might be yet another visit ahead. I would recommend going at least four times and staying for a week if you can afford the time to get a sense of the community.

Other Things to Think About

Depending on your industry, weather may be a consideration. It's a big factor for me, as I am in the business of making mild steel and stainless steel fasteners. Illinois is humid. Mississippi is humid. I still look almost daily and compare temperatures, real feel, and yes, humidity. Mississippi runs twenty to thirty degrees warmer, but our humidity runs about the same, and often Illinois is higher. However, my steel rusts almost as fast as it is produced. My cardboard boxes need a special storage place, as I cannot just leave them to face the open air since they wilt. The inventory boxes on my shelves fall apart. The labels on my inventory fade and fall off, so we are regularly relabeling.

Available housing is another consideration. This was nowhere in the vicinity of my brain to consider. I simply assumed that there is rental property. There is rental property in my location. Sadly, only a small portion of apartments are in a good part of town. The houses for rent are in rough shape and very expensive. My current task is convincing the county to lower its taxes on second homes/rental properties with strings attached so that the home owners can tend to the houses.

Another discovery I have made is that, while our team members know the handbook policy and legal policy much better than myself, they do not necessarily know how to manage a rental agreement. Why is this important? If you go to a place like Clarksdale or Blytheville, your accessibility to skilled labor for your business needs is limited. I have recruited from outside the area and have brought in to find out that there is a housing shortage. Some folks roll with what the area has to offer; other folks drive thirty to ninety minutes.

What does the county tax and how much? Specifically look for an economic development tax. This will allow you to get financial assistance from the county for any expansion projects. Huge if you want to expand your facility or do some construction within your facility. As long as you are bringing in jobs, you will get funding. Three years later, we are looking at a new division. We figure it will require ten more employees, a paint booth, and some other construction to fit the new line. We estimated the project to be about $265,000 to 300,000. We brought in EDC and ACE grant folks. Yep, no problem.

Another location consideration is if it is eligible for any other federal grants. We are located in one of the poorest counties in the USA. However, it afforded us the opportunity to apply and get a federal grant called New Market Tax Credits. This is a crazy grant and extraordinarily complicated, far more complicated than your typical grant process. However, it essentially allowed us to borrow three million dollars at an extremely low interest rate, i.e. one percent, and repay only two million. Yes, you got it: keep one million.

Our location is also in a HUBZone, which is only for communities that are considered historically underutilized business. You have to apply, and because it is a government program, it has a lot of red tape. However, the government already has outlined that if you are conducting business in "x" location, you are HUBZone eligible. The goal of HUBZone is for companies in these locations to be awarded a minimum of 3 percent of federal contract dollars per year.

Government entities at both Federal and State levels have to meet certain requirements. They have to spend so many dollars with underprivileged organizations. Women-owned businesses used to be huge, but now that women are claiming their rights in the world, not such a big deal. However, the HUBZone is rarely met. It brings you right up to the top of the award list.

Also do your homework on internet infrastructure and capacity. In today's world, we are handcuffed by internet availability. We did vet this, and Clarksdale has amazing internet. Why? We did not know, nor did we care. I now know why. The poorer the community, the more they use or rely on the internet. Facebook is huge. It makes no sense to me.

Secondary and raw material suppliers: can you replace your current outsourced suppliers easily? Being in northern Illinois, which is a very dense manufacturing area, I was very spoiled in outside support being readily available. I knew Clarksdale would not, but I thought for sure that the larger, closer cities would have viable options. Cities such as Memphis and Nashville in Tennessee; or Little Rock, Arkansas; or Jackson and Hattiesburg, Mississippi; or Birmingham, Alabama; or Houston and Forth Worth and Dallas, Texas; or Missouri. I was wrong. I had to continue to run parts to Illinois, and as it ended up, they were actually the closest options. Gratefully, our facility is so large that we were able to invest in equipment to eliminate almost all of our outsourced secondary operations. This is both good and bad. Good in that we had full control over our production. Bad in that we had to uplevel our skills in order to operate all the new equipment.

Can you readily get your raw materials from your suppliers? That answer will be yes. What I mean is you must consider the expense of transit time, transit cost, and transit loss of product. For instance, I purchase a large amount of raw materials from a company that used to be able to deliver to us. With the move, their delivery charge was so high, understandably, but I had to outsource full truck loads. Essentially, I had to take over the logistics of that supplier. It is fine, but it took me a minute to figure out how to do this reasonably—both in terms of cost and transit time.

Logistics for the site needs to be evaluated, if for no other reason that you are prepared. If you are located in a rural area and even right off the highway, like us, it doesn't matter. No trucking company wants to come to you daily. I am fortunate enough to have developed a good relationship with a few drivers and use them daily either via outbound or inbound shipments that they will come in every day. We are gaining more traction after three years. But if you want a shipment to go out and it is 2:00 p.m., and it is not on a carrier that is already coming in, guess what? It is not going out. Period. Salespeople and customers don't believe me. Believe me.

We need to discuss expenses. If you have ever done a remodel, you know that the estimated price is always short of the actual by about 30 percent, actually. Know that the same is true for your move. We were awarded $3,000,000 in grant money and ended up putting in 30 percent beyond that. Crazy, I know. But as in every remodel, unexpected factors often arise. This book will hopefully help you. But I have spoken to remodelers, and even though that is their livelihood, they have told me that all projects work out to be this magical 30 percent over budget.

At this point, you have to decide: stay or go. One last item needs to be explored. Go back to your town and county's economic development and see if they will offer anything to keep you. I would also check out nearby counties to see what they would offer to have you. Like I said earlier, I had an open mindset to this move, and I did not have to go looking. I already had other local counties coming to me with move packages. The village of Huntley basically told us to go pound sand. The sad reality is if they had offered just $10,000 off our insanely high taxes, we probably would have taken it instead of uprooting our life, our company, and our employees.

When I relocated, I did not consider my personal life enough. This was all about the company. It is truly my one regret that I went into this with eyes wide shut. I assumed I would find a barn that would be agreeable for me and my horses. After all, I was in the south. The partners of economic development all told me that I could board my horses locally. That was not the case. The local vet is the sweetest man, and he gave me names and numbers for folks that had horses. I called all of them, and only one seemed to be interested and able to board.

I would be giving up a riding arena, but he offered his farmland to go trail riding, so I was like, done. While we were chatting, he received multiple texts and a call from his wife, and later that night at midnight, he texted that he was very sorry, but he could not take my horse in for board. Sometimes it pays to be attractive and other times not so much. I do have him boarded by my house outside of Memphis, but I have given up the ability to ride whenever I want as there is no covered arena. I no longer show. Dog training down here is different as well. Up north, there are kennel clubs where you can take you and your dog for obedience training, agility, and a myriad of other sports. That is not the case here.

How big is your village? How good are you at rebuilding that village? My village was vast. Being a female, building a solid and trustworthy community takes time. Going south, building a village is not impossible, but it certainly is not easy. The men told me that they have a women in business club down here. Get this: the name is the gardening club. I am all about it. If you are male, building a village in the south will certainly not be a problem. If you are female, building a village in the north is easier than the south.

I am not saying it is not possible; it just takes what I now call a "southern minute" to do that. Yes, a "southern minute" is a phrase I coined after moving here. Up north, if I asked someone to do something and they said, "sure, in a minute," that meant within a few minutes. Down here, a minute could be days. I asked one of my supervisors, "Where is my information? You told me you would get it for me in a minute, and it has been days." He looked at me a bit surprised and said, "Yes, a minute. That could mean a minute to a week." I was a bit shocked.

Now I say, "I need this information in a northern minute" if I need it right away, or I will say a "southern minute will be fine." Everyone laughs—but the message is received and understood.

Chapter 4
How to Vet the Workforce

It is only through labor and painful effort, by grim energy, and resolute courage, that we move on to better things.

—Theodore Roosevelt

Had I known then what I know now . . . famous last words. My mindset regarding the vetting of the workforce would be totally different. I did not understand how poverty, community make up, crime levels, and community culture radically affect your hiring model. I, like every established business owner, have really never had to think about it.

First thing you need to know is the labor availability. I do not mean skilled labor. If you are going to a more affluent area, then you might find skilled labor options. Given today's labor shortage—not even skilled labor shortage– is unlikely that any community will follow through with skilled labor. In order to determine the labor availability, get some stats on the community.

First stat: what is the unemployment rate of the community as well as the county? If the unemployment rate is less than 5 percent, you will have a tough time finding labor. It is my opinion that a certain percentage of the population are unemployable. A million reasons exist for people to not work. I personally think that when you get to 3 percent unemployment rate, the rest of the population is not employable.

What is the percentage of people at poverty level? A key statistic here is how long the level has been held? What I did not know is that while 70 percent of my community is at poverty level, I did not do the math on how long that large percentage had been at poverty level. It didn't dawn on me until I was really struggling with recruiting and retention that the community was in third generation poverty. Sad, yes, but what does this mean?

This means that the majority of people do not know how to work. This concept is so huge I am repeating it again. The majority of people in third generation poverty do not know *how* to work. They do not have the advantages of being in a home or school environment where they have mentors of some type to demonstrate how to work. Their parents don't work nor do their grandparents. This is not a deal breaker, but it changed how I hire. I did not understand this until I was a year into massive employee turnover drama.

People want to work. They want to feel good about themselves. Unfortunately, the system is set up against them and us as employers. Most communities or counties have displaced worker grants, but the grant requirements are tough to meet. They want these displaced workers to be employed full time. I would too. It is not in their capacity to do this. More than likely, they have never held a full time job; they probably don't know anyone who has or does have a job; their support system is composed of people like them, so basically no support.

Yes, they like the paycheck, but they struggle with all the rules that we take for granted as we have been doing them all our lives. I am currently working with the local policy makers to reach the government legislators who make the rules but have no street experience. I would love for all these people to be off the system. I think everyone would.

Worse, this is the reason we were solicited so heavily to the areas where the unemployment rate is high. The government sees the financial potential on so many levels by getting these folks off the system. However, the problem is that the grant dollars, which make it easier for people like us to get the unemployable hired, have such stringent rules. They will only pay if you hire them full time. Since these folks have no clue how to do work, it will always fail. You hire them, taking advantage of the grant money only to fire them within thirty to sixty days because of poor attendance, quality, and productivity issues. More than likely, you and your managers don't know they are part of the "unemployable" category either. At the end of the day, it doesn't matter, as you have to get the product shipped.

My solution for this is that you hire them and only ask them to show up three days a week for an hour starting sometime after 10:00 a.m., give them an easy task to do, and pay them in cash at the end of the hour. Repeat until they get this part down. We need to help them start building that muscle. It is not going to happen with an eight hour shift. Further, this muscle-building process is extraordinarily slow.

If you are dealing with a person who has not held a job for more than three months—not six, I will get into that later—you are more than likely dealing with someone who is in generational poverty. They are not going to show up every day at 6:00 a.m. They are not going to be back from break or lunch on time. Remember, they are very charming because that is what life has taught them. This is how they survive. They will tell you adamantly how badly they need a job, and they are believable because they do indeed need a job. It is my belief that they also really want to work. Perhaps that mindset is my burden, but I truly believe that, which is probably why I survived.

I equate this situation to someone who wants to lose weight. They view it as a diet, not as a lifestyle change. In order to lose weight and successfully keep it off, you must have a lifestyle change of choosing different foods. Diets don't work because in our psyche, it is a temporary state of mind. When you first start said diet, it is *hard*—really *hard*. You have to think differently when you eat. You have to create your grocery list differently. You have to think when you go grocery shopping and read labels versus just grabbing food. Most people fail at diets because it is hard and they have not developed the muscle to manage the change they desire.

This is similar to employment. At the end of the day, both situations involve underdeveloped muscles and are difficult to follow through. All you have is your own mindset, and if you have had no mindset training and no support system to help you reach your goals, which many don't, failure is likely.

What is the makeup of the community?

What is the ethnicity of the community you hire within? I personally do not care if you are purple with pink polka dots as long as you show up and do your job. Yes, I knew that my workforce would be black. I did not care. I am not prejudiced. If you have an issue with the ethnicity of the community, do not move there. People are smart and can be underestimated. If it bothers you, people will know. As a new employer, you are watched like a hawk.

What I missed was that a lot of my workforce cared that we were white. Every time I turned around, I was being called a racist. I have never been called racist, and my workforce up north was Hispanic. I was the minority due to the community in which the facility was located. I totally missed this critical piece. I do believe that this bias can be overcome in training, which I will get to in a later chapter.

A funny story, though—let me preface it by advising that my patience was beginning to wear. I had a black female team member and a white male team member. She was caught smoking in the plant, and everyone knows smoking in the plant is not allowed. She got written up for it. He apparently was smoking too, but nobody caught him. She accused me of being racist, and I was not even the one who caught her or wrote her up. I told her that it had nothing to do with racism. If you are going to break the rules, then you need to be smarter about it. As the words left my mouth, I was actually in shock that I said them.

What is the crime rate?

Communities where the offering is rich typically have a high crime rate. I am in a high crime rate county. I knew this going in. I am a firm believer in second-chance employment, and I looked at it as an opportunity. Quite honestly, with the current labor shortage, every employer needs to be a second-chance employer. Historically, I have hired and retained a fair amount of second- chance employees with great success. I am proud of myself for this.

What I failed to do the math on was how much of the community is gang driven. This is not information you will get from economic development, as they may have an idea, but I don't know that they would be able to quantify it, and if they could, it would be presented with roses. That is their job. Again, I don't care about the community being overrun by gangs—within the scope of employment, that is. It would have been helpful to know that, though, as it would have seriously changed my hiring strategy.

Another question to do a deep dive on is what are the mayor and chief of police doing about the crime rate. Are they on the same page? Do they have a team actively working on pushing that crime rate down? Where have they been trending over the past five plus years? *How* will your business help with the crime statistics? *Will* your business help with the crime statistics? They should have the answers to these questions. I'd recommend having multiple meetings with the mayor and doing your homework.

What is the unemployment rate?

If the unemployment rate is 5 percent or less, I believe that it will be tough to build a workforce as you are only dealing with 2 percent of the population as viable potential employees. If you know the percentage at poverty level, the crime percentage, the unemployment rate, you will have a rough idea of the pool of the population that are potential employees. I did not know that then, but I know it now. The unemployment rate was so high in my area that I thought this was a no-brainer. Had I known the information from earlier in this chapter, I would have been successful much faster.

Where is the population of available labor?

Every single economic development person told me that people will drive up to fifty minutes for a job. I was hesitant to believe this, but they advised me that in the rural areas, people would drive for more pay. I figure that this was probably true due to the lack of industry in the rural counties.

Friends, I am here to tell you, this is simply not true. People will not drive that distance to work, and the money doesn't matter. Well, it might. If you have skilled labor and you are paying them as such, then they may drive. However, I have a roster of fifty-three, and only two drive any kind of distance. The one complains about it loudly and almost daily. Yes, he could move but there is the housing issue, which I explained previously. You can count on people driving twenty minutes, and depending on where you set up shop, that could be twenty miles if you are in a rural location.

Chapter 5
Can the Community Step Up to the Training Needs

Every enterprise is a learning and teaching institution. Training and development must be built into it on all levels—training and development that never stop.

—Peter Drucker

Workforce Development Support

It is imperative that you take a deep dive into what and how much workforce development is able and willing to do to help in this lift. You need to evaluate if the community not only has the capacity but also the capability, and if they don't, can you work with them to shore it up. Again, the communities that are in the most need will step up more than the communities that don't really need to get people employed.

First let's look at capacity. Capacity defined is the ability or power to do, experience, or understand something. Does workforce development have the ability and the power to understand your needs fully? Can you explain to them in detail your needs? Can you quantify exactly the skill set you need to have in order to train people to do the job? I ask these pointed questions because it will only help you to help workforce development help you. It is a "how can I help you help me" question. The higher job levels function in the white-collar world and have no idea what skills are needed for any kind of manufacturing job unless they themselves came from that world, which is probably unlikely.

People's skillset declines as you get to the more financially challenged towns. However, that does not mean that people cannot be trained. We had trained over 300 people at this point in time. Just because people are in a poverty stricken area does not mean that they cannot learn. I have spoken to several more prominent people in the community and am absolutely shocked when they ask me "can *they* be trained?" Yes, Clarksdale public education is extraordinarily poor, and thank goodness I am not someone who believes that you need to go to school to succeed in life. Will always wins over quantified intelligence—at least in my book.

On the flip side, when you go to a more desirable location, the labor shortage may adversely affect the employment options. You might find the trade or skill set needed for your workforce, but they are probably already hired. You would have to poach other companies, and depending on the community, this might not go over so well.

People like the status quo. They do not necessarily want to change jobs because no one likes change. In order to successfully poach, you need to have an incredible offer of money and incentives, and that is no guarantee the employee will stay for even six months.

Capacity - Can you and workforce development work together to create a viable workforce for your organization?

Second is capability. Capability is defined as the power or ability to do something. Can your workforce development deliver what you need?

Chapter 5

Do they have the power to say *yes*, we can do this. Or *yes*, we don't know how, but we will figure it out. Are they willing to get in the trenches with you?

Our lift was big. Only seven of our forty-six employees moved with us. The county's workforce development brought in Fanuc control panels for us. They found a CNC programmer to give CNC training classes so that when folks hit the floor for hands-on training, they were at least familiar with the operation. They started an essential skills training program. They have paid for leadership programs—as they didn't have any—to further improve the communication skill set for our team members. They endorsed our quality training program. They will do whatever they can to help us improve the skills of our employees.

This is what you need, and in my opinion, it is what every company needs. They need the support of the local workforce development. I could get this back in Illinois, but it was not easy. The rules and regulations that I had to jump through for approval were challenging. Further, Illinois itself, along with many counties, were financially challenged in receiving funding for these efforts.

Along with capacity and capability is financial willingness. Our lift was much larger than we had anticipated it to be and much larger than the state anticipated it to be. If I had known then what I know now, I could have significantly improved that, but I did not, and nor did workforce development. At the end of the day, training is costly. Worth it, but costly. Is the county behind you 100 percent, or are they only invested in the signature line of your relocation? Meaning, will they stick with you and your needs or not?

I had many interviews with many folks in workforce development from the state, county, and community levels, and there is a huge difference in communication from location to location. For many of the places we vetted, the place was good—but the workforce development, not so much. What turned out to be a profound question for me was, "What are you willing to do to provide training for my heading department?"

Full training for cold heading takes over a year. It takes someone six months to be somewhat competent. Are you willing to pay for people to come and train at my facility? Get deep with them. You will know by their answers and body language if they are a "can do" or a "geez, I am not sure if I can do."

When I sat down with Coahoma county, the president said to me, "Can we buy one of these cold heading machines and put it in our training department?" I was a bit floored and said, "Well, yes, but it is not like they are inexpensive." She said, "Give me a number," and I said, "Well, cheap—like really cheap—is $250,000." She said, "Okay."

Right? *That* is engagement. *That* is a leader who thinks outside the box to promote community.

How do you know they will put their money where their mouth is? Look at it as any other business deal. There is that gut feel, that knowing of hell yes or hell no. I promise, you will know by their body posture and verbiage. You will know if they have both the capacity and the capability to step up or not.

Training Support

When inquiring about training, consider what training the community has or has access to currently. Some communities don't cross share unless you ask. Say you need automotive repair, and the county you are considering does not have it. Ask about other community colleges or training centers. It always amazes me how people do not think beyond their current situation. I tell my customer service team that you often need to think of alternatives beyond what the customer may ask or see. We cannot do this, but we can offer you this instead. Often, it works out. Be prepared to brainstorm solutions for the community, which is really for yourself.

What new programs are they looking at bringing into the college or training center? Do any of those align with your needs? This also gives you an idea of what is trending in your community. Is it a transferable skill? For instance, Coahoma county is predominantly an agricultural county. The workforce development college is working on developing a diesel engine training program. Is a diesel engine mechanic a transferable skill? Big yes for us and probably a big yes for all the other manufacturer's out there.

Can and will they bring in training aids to help train for your needed skills? The college brought in Fanuc control boards. When I did my quality training, they offered to buy the quality instruments for the training. What is it that they are able and willing to do for you? It is your job to act as an investigative reporter and ask a lot of questions. Step out of your box and act as if the world is your oyster. What are your dream training wants?

Next Steps

After you have done all your vetting, visiting the locations, dived deep with workforce development, you need to decide to move forward with a move or uplevel where you are currently. As after this experience, you can really never go back, as you have now been forever changed. Been forever changed even if you don't move? Yes. This touring of communities and interviewing workforce development will broaden your perspective. If you decide not to move or open a new division, you will think about recruiting, retaining, and workforce development in a whole new light.

If you are uncertain about recruiting, don't do it. Labor is hard enough to find in today's market.

When I was on this path, I knew which locations would have a viable workforce and which ones wouldn't. I distinctly remember sitting in a meeting with the director of economic development for Coahoma county and his expression when he was trying to sell me on workforce availability. I flatly told him, "Oh, I am not worried about labor availability." He was stunned. But I knew I would have ample labor in this community. I wish I had also known other things, but I knew it, and I was correct. To this day, I get at least twenty-five job applications a week. Granted, most of these people want to keep unemployment benefits or are working the system, but in that weekly stack, there are a handful of good people who need and deserve a job.

At this stage, we decided that we needed to make sure that our very top and key people knew and were on board with this potential decision. I would have brought them in sooner, but we have married couples that worked for us, and obviously they would have to discuss this with their spouse. When we spilled the news, they were not really surprised. It was a bit surreal. But then again, they didn't like Illinois either.

Now, I think there will always be uncertainty. However, with any major business or life decision, there is uncertainty. I was uncertain, but I also knew I had to do something drastically different with the company if I wanted to really compete with the giants in my industry. Even with ten plus patents, at the end of the day, we sell steel fasteners, and it is a volume- and priced-based industry. I remember "signing day." We had

Chapter 5

made some changes within the family structure, which alleviated much of the cash pressure to pay for the taxes. On that day, my brother came into my office for me to sign the documents, and I said, "We don't have to do this move." And after my experience of the first two years, I wished I had not signed. Those two years were the most difficult of my entire life.

Again, I am writing this book so that if you decide to take the plunge, you have guidance. Had I known any of the rest of this book, those two years would have been completely different.

Since you will have uncertainty, sort out how much of it is fear based or is your gut telling you something different. For me, when I know, I know. It is generally easier for women to get into this space of gut feeling or intuition. However, I believe that the majority of successful entrepreneurs just know when they know. It is an undeniable force that lies within all of us; it simply takes over and brings a certain clarity with it.

The other thing I knew about Clarksdale is that not only would I be able to recruit a viable workforce, but that they would actually be better than the workforce I had in Illinois. Now, why I thought this, I have no clue. I was trading a workforce of twenty some years for a new workforce. What was I thinking, right? But here we are three years later with a workforce that is predominantly one to two years old, almost to the expertise of veteran Illinois people. This is nothing short of astonishing.

Dig down in your soul: are you signing or not? If the answer is no, continue to read, as you will still gain many insights about workforce development, courage, and tenacity through the rest of the book. If the answer is yes, then read on, as this is really where the journey begins.

Press Release

The community will be super excited that you have signed. They will want a press release right away. My recommendation is to not let them drive this ship. There are many things to consider with a press release, mostly your current team members. Clarksdale MS is 900 miles from Huntley, Illinois. How would a local press release remotely get back to your team? In this day and age, you cannot bank that it won't. You need to have a few things managed before you allow the press release.

Chapter 6
How to Manage the Existing Workforce

Comfort is the enemy of achievement.

—Farrah Gray

I completely underestimated my existing workforce. Well, actually I completely underestimated human nature and the fear of change. Clearly, I am a risk taker. Growth comes from change. Change is a regular occurrence in any entrepreneurial mindset. I understood that this was scary, but the move provided an opportunity for our team members to leave the third most moved out of state for a much friendlier tax environment with job security and some extra cash.

After we told our team, I had long conversations with a department supervisor, as he wanted to buy a house. He had four children. Two lived with him and expected his daughter from his previous relationship to move in as well. All was good until we talked about the taxes. Illinois property taxes are like another mortgage, making his dream of a white picket fence extraordinarily difficult. Actually, the property taxes made it unobtainable. I explained that in Mississippi, real estate taxes were literally a fraction of the cost.

That closed the deal for him, but not his wife. His wife absolutely refused to move. She used every excuse possible: my children need to learn Spanish; I need to get my translation certificate; I need to see my mother every Wednesday and Saturday. The list went on, and as a natural problem solver, I overcame all her obstacles. As a moving bonus, We offered to pay their house downpayment. No dice.

Contracts

I highly recommend that you are prepared with retention contracts. What are you going to offer for those who do not move? You have to offer something, or they will walk. That retention contract needs to handcuff them to their job with you. Most people will want to get another job right away. This is a normal human reaction, so expect it, and be prepared to say, "Wait a minute."

The contract needs to lay out the expectations very specifically. You need to put in a date of how long you expect to need them and reinforce that this is a guestimate, but you will give them two weeks' notice should that date change. You must emphasize that you will be in communication with them regularly. This information needs to walk the floor regularly so that people feel comfortable and do not think you have abandoned them.

You need them to continue to produce as well as train the new workforce. Money, and enough of it, is the only thing you have that they want. Also, be prepared for your scrap rates to go up. We were at about 1 percent scrap rate, and it shot up to 6 percent during this transition. Again, this is one of the reasons why I mentioned previously to put six to nine months of inventory on your floor.

You will need to schedule one-on-one conversations to determine where people stand and what challenges they face and how you as the employer can help them overcome those challenges. In one of the one-on-one conversations, you must also discuss each person's willingness to come and train in your new location. This is critical, and it is another negotiated retention piece.

Being in Illinois or any other state where many employment laws exist, you have to be same same. Meaning you have to treat all your employees the same with the bonus structure of the move package or they can sue you. We did our "stay on" package based on years of service and current pay. We did 10 percent for years five and over, then went on a sliding scale from there. You want all your employees to move with you. They won't. If you have an employee that you want to move with you and stay on, give them a raise before this hits, and do it several months earlier, even if you are uncertain of a move. Look, if they are important enough to you, they deserve the raise anyway. This way, the state cannot accuse you of unfair labor practice when you create move packages. Our retention contracts cost us about $100,000 for the thirty-nine employees who did not move. We also had a few—only one or two—employees who left us anyway, regardless of the retention bonus.

Conversely, if the employee moves with you, you don't have to have same same across the board. We planned on having one-on-one conversations with each employee to determine if we needed to start taking other action. We needed to be prepared and rise to the occasion in managing their needs. Also, do note that people's needs are not as substantial as you think. I was shocked by what people needed in order to move. Some needed rent money, some needed a U-Haul truck—everyone's needs were much less than what I had expected. Be prepared to offer pay increases and relate that to the cost of living in your new location. Many people need assistance in translating what a raise means in their "new" life.

Now if the employee(s) are not going to move with you but are willing to move for a short time period, again it does not need to be same same for labor law compliance. For those folks, at this point, I could have easily converted them to 1099 contractors. I did not because I did not want to jeopardize their health care benefits. I gave substantial raises to these people. I found and paid for housing indefinitely. I was blessed and will be forever grateful to the few folks that stayed on anywhere from six months to eighteen months. Without their help, we would not have made it.

In Clarksdale, or any impoverished town, a raise goes much further simply because of a lower cost of living in the new location. People don't understand what that really means. We did a spreadsheet of old costs versus new costs and how much more money that they would have in their pocket at the end of the day.

How do you tell your team?

Well for one thing, your team already knows something is up. Your employees watch you and what you do far more than you realize. Anything off or out of the norm, and they immediately know. Once, I had an employee ask me why I wasn't wearing red boots. I was like, "What?" He said, "You are wearing a red top, and you always wear red boots to match, and today you didn't. Why?"

We put together a PowerPoint presentation along with a move package, which included the retention contracts. We began with the hardship that Illinois presented and how costly it was to live and be profitable there. Then we dropped the bomb. The employees reported that when they saw the packets, they knew it wasn't good. Whatever was coming, was not good.

We of course addressed the crime issue upfront, as when you google Clarksdale, Mississippi, it is bad. They have made great strides in the last five years, but a bad element has a good foothold on that community, and it will take time to chip it down. We talked about the cost of living, which is much less than Illinois. Car fuel, food, utilities, and real estate are all substantially less. We presented an analysis for the difference in cost of living from McHenry county to Coahoma county and translated that into how much more money would be in their pocket versus the governments. Financially this was a no-brainer. Financially, it offered our folks the affordability of actually buying a house and living the American dream.

We had already scheduled people for one-on-one interviews three days after the announcement. This allowed them to somewhat recover from the shock as well as to discuss with their families. We wanted to get a temperature check of where people stood. 50 percent of them said they would seriously consider this and wanted more information. Now, I knew I was not going to get 50 percent of them to come. I only had one reference, and that was from a business owner who moved his company out of Crystal Lake, Illinois to Tennessee in 2012. He told us that 30 percent of his team moved with him. This was my benchmark, as I could not find any other data. A few weeks later, we had another round of interviews, and the number of people moving had dropped to 30 percent.

We took those 30 percent and their significant others road tripping to Clarksdale, Mississippi. We showed them the good areas of Clarksdale, as well as other viable communities to live and call home. We did a night in Memphis, which was a blast. Memphis is only one hour and twenty minutes from Clarksdale. We toured the plant and showed where everything would be set up. Where they would work. We had the mayor answer questions about the community. We had several other prominent figures of the town share their thoughts on Clarksdale. They were asked some tough questions about the community, crime, and future plans. Everyone had a great time, and we got to know people in a very different way.

Due note that the community picked up the tab on this trip. Another item that we negotiated in the package.

Sadly, after the trip, we dropped to 15 percent. I underestimated the "family" bond in the Latino community. I had one woman tell me that she had to see her mother every weekend if not every day. I had others that were interested in moving, or so they said, but had family members that would not even consider it. I am talking about cousin types of family members, not like spouses. To make things still more difficult, I could only convince a handful of people to go down for training purposes. It seemed to be a huge deal for people to leave their home base for a week.

In retrospect, I would have handled the distance training differently. Out the gate, I would have offered them double pay to go down for a week at a time to train. Obviously room is paid and a dollar food reimbursement with a max daily allowance. I am confident that that would have elicited a different response. I was thinking people would negotiate but no such luck. Another oversight on my part. You and I, we know that everything is negotiable. The people on your plant floor don't think anything is negotiable, unless of course they have been around the block.

Now, I do not know if this is a cultural thing or a fuck you thing. Several of my Caucasian folks came down for months, not even on a week on and week off deal. They just packed up and came down. I was able to rent a house for several of them and a hotel for others. I only had two Hispanic team members come down for lengths of time. I really truly liked my team, but we had ripped the ground out from underneath them, or so they thought. People do not like change. Initially, I thought their lack of engagement to come and train was cultural, but after being there for six months, I had two previous employees reach out to see if we were still in business. This leads me to believe that it was a fuck you move. I underestimated Latino culture, but they underestimated my drive.

Employee Support

My team was and is very important to me. The company and I would not be where we are without their efforts. I know some owners do not agree with me, even in today's labor market, or lack thereof. When I talk about support, I am talking about both employees who are moving with you and not moving with you. Either way, it is a massive change in their worlds.

I prominently listed the mental health help hotline that our insurance company offers. Most insurance companies have a mental health hotline and counseling. The hotlines are obviously free of charge, and counseling is also typically free of charge, but that is per the health care plan.

I also found a life coach that took our insurance. I posted her number and advised people how life coaches work—I am one, after all. It does not matter if people actually reach out to get emotional support. What matters is that you cared enough to do the research and to advise them.

What are you going to do to help your remaining team members get another job? Now, I realize that the labor market is tight, and folks will not have a tough time getting employed, but they did not. Many of them were terrified of being unemployed and losing benefits. I did want them to make just as much if not more money with another company. I assured my people that I would help them get another job if they stayed on. I did not put this in writing in the retention package on purpose. I did not want to get sued because they continually turned down jobs for whatever reason.

I realize that I went overboard, but their retention and production was so important that I pulled out all the stops. I actually created a resume for all my hourly personnel. It was not hard by any means, but it was extraordinarily time consuming. I reached out to local businesses and interviewed their HR person. I advised what was happening with me and asked about their pay rates and hiring practices. Depending on their response, I posted details—company, location, starting pay range, as well as if they were an E-Verify company. I don't know for certain, but I would not be surprised if I had a few illegal folks on my team. I was not an E-Verify company, and as long as they had provided the necessary documentation, I was fine.

I also reached out to the county's workforce development center to advise them that I was going to have a mass layoff. They came in with their computers and had interviews with each employee to get them in their database for employers who were looking for labor through that channel.

The tricky thing was to convince my team members that they could get a job with a postponed start date. I told them that they were special and that companies will wait. Further, the companies that I worked with were all very accommodating, as I was being very nice, and nobody wants to see you fail after a favor. Most were happy with their new position because nobody took a pay cut, and a few received a pay increase.

It was an incredibly grueling process for me, as it was very demanding in both time and mental energy. My team members had no idea the amount of work that went into all that, and I honestly don't know that they were grateful. Some were for certain, but most were not. If I were to do this again, I would not do their resumes. I would most certainly reach out to other employers, etc., and obviously I would offer emotional support information.

Chapter 7
Rebuilding your Workforce

I will take anyone who is motivated and has initiative anyday over someone who did well on their ACT, work keys tests.

—Stacia Hobson

I did not view it as rebuilding my workforce. I viewed it as hiring forty new employees. This perspective kept me out of overwhelm but also lessened the significance of recruiting. I allowed higher levels of workforce development to take over driving much of this because really I had no other choice to my knowledge. This would have been fine had I known that they did not understand their own workforce situation. I thought that they understood their community. I missed that while they talked a good game, they had no handle on it.

They thought people would drive forty-five minutes for good employment. Wrong. They thought that all the people in the community would be grateful for fifty new jobs. Wrong. I was easily led to believe that people were on some type of government aid because there was such a lack of industry. Wrong. Wong. Wrong.

Again, it really depends on the size of the community. The smaller the community, the more important the next segment is for you.

Coahoma county has only 20,000 people, and Clarksdale's population is 14,000. This is small. Furthermore, Clarksdale is very rural. We are approximately an hour and a half south of Memphis, which is the closest largest city. Getting references from employees and integrating yourself into the community as fast as possible is what matters. It is who you know, not what you provide.

You can provide jobs paying over $18 per hour for unskilled labor, and trust me, it does not matter. One clue that I missed in what it really meant was when I interviewed the previous general manager of the company that had been in or building. He continually repeated that everyone was family. The previous employees called it family. What I have been taught is that family means family. If one employee has an issue, we all have an issue and must rally to help that person. This takes my "no team member left behind" thinking to a whole new level.

I had an employee whose pipes burst at her apartment. Work ceased until a resolution had been reached and until people donated enough money to help her out of her situation.

To date, it is difficult for me to refer to our team as our family. I have been a northerner too long, resulting in my acknowledgement that I am still a work in progress. I step up and help where I can when someone is down. I give far more leeway here than I did up north, and it has paid off.

Community Integration

Another aspect that I never thought about is community integration. How do you integrate yourself and your company into the community? You need to do things that reach your potential workforce, literally when you sign that contract. Things like give an iPad to each fifth grader at a public school. Get your Facebook page up and post *daily* about your community involvement, what you are doing, and the progress of your move and your hiring. Get locals to like the Facebook page and to comment on it. While Coahoma county is the poorest county in Mississippi, it is the largest user of the internet. Now, this does not mean that folks are internet savvy. They use Facebook as a means of communication.

Another way to integrate yourself is to sponsor community events. Now, it was suggested that I sponsor one of the festivals that Clarksdale is known for, but a better strategy is to go to the local high school and sponsor their football, basketball, whatever teams. They need money for trips, for uniforms, and the like. *That* will make an impression on your audience. Donating to the food bank is another way to make an impression. Whatever your community needs, fill and advertise the crap out of it.

I received a huge lesson in marketing. I used to provide uniforms for my team. They paid zero. It was a good deal for them. Uniform providers are scam artists in my experience. The company I used was charging me $300 in rags a week and yet only dropping off sixteen rags on some weeks, claiming that we did not have any to pick up the week before. Folks, I am a cold heading shop. Oil is not our middle name, but our first. It got to the point where I made the driver weigh in and out rags and sign off on them. I also made them sign off on uniform returns as they kept charging me for uniforms that had been previously returned and then denying receipt. Oh my word—I was pissed. I fired them.

I decided to buy our folks T-shirts and then offer them the opportunity to buy additional ones if they wanted. This paid off huge and in ways I never dreamed possible. First and foremost, my team members liked the tees better than the uniforms. They are more comfortable and breathe so much better during those unbelievably hot days.

Second, it was free advertising. The only real store we have here is Walmart. My first shift gets off at 2:30 p.m. They go shopping. I cannot tell you how many team members told me that they were stopped because people saw the Image shirts and wanted to know how they liked working at Image. This was a game changer for my hiring a year ago. Again, this was an extraordinary way of getting your name out into the community.

First Hires

Make it a mission to hire a general. Act as if you are going to a foreign country and you need someone to speak the language. After six months, my CNC production supervisor advised that he could not move permanently because his wife was no bueno, even though I offered to buy them a house. She could not leave her family. I explained to them that the likelihood of them being able to have a home in Illinois was slim simply due to the property taxes being like another mortgage. Fell on deaf ears.

At any rate, we recruited a new supervisor. He had zero CNC experience, but he had supervisory experience and had workforce connections. People trusted him. He has been in the community for years. He knew most of our workforce already. He sat me down after two months and said that we had to clean the house. We cannot move forward with what we have going on right now. He was right. While many were good producers, they did not care about quality. They did not care about the job. They did not care about the company. They certainly did not think about longevity. We had fifty-five employees,

Chapter 7

and in a matter of eighteen months, churned—wait for it—200 people. Now, had we had someone like him helping in the hiring process, we could have cut down that churn to under a year and probably down to fifty-five people instead of two hundred.

If you can hire a human resource generalist, do it. I hired a guy that was moving to be with his family in a town nearby, but he really did not have the depth of experience needed for what we were undertaking. Now, hiring was crazy because I took advantage of the state-funded programs, which were paperwork-intensive and confusing. Then COVID hit, and the government agencies closed to the public, which meant that we had to take on all the paperwork. Regardless, I had to let him go.

Sadly, many of the folks hired had drug dependencies. He tested one, and they were positive. I had to disregard my no tolerance policy initially because everyone would have been fired. At any rate, the team member tested positive. He admitted he had taken something, so I said that he needed to be sent home. The HR person sent him on his way, meaning allowed him to drive. I couldn't believe what he had done. I said, "Well, I won't call you if I am drunk since you will tell me to get in my car and drive." I was explicit that it is our responsibility to see that the employee either gets a ride or that we get them a ride moving forward. Yet, he did it again. I let him go and explained to MDES the situation and that he was a liability.

However, if you can find a HR generalist from the area or one that understands the area, they would be in your best interest to recruit and get on your team. I tried again and again to fill this role with no luck. Paperwork and accountability are huge in the HR realm, and if you don't have anyone on top of that, then you will have issues with unemployment security. In my case, as we fired so many people, it is certainly a reason to draw attention. I have to say that I am pretty proud of having fired over 200 people in a three year period. I have only lost three unemployment claims. Two of those were beyond my control. One was the fact that we were not notified of the hearing, and the other was that the judge was biased. Yes, of course I say that, right? Here is the deal. I have always had several couples working for me. Since moving to Mississippi, I have had several situations where I have rethought this hiring process. This is one of them.

We had a boyfriend and girlfriend working for us. They both just stopped showing up to work. No call, no show. He had a tardiness problem, but tardiness and no show are very different. This was not normal behavior for her. We finally heard from the guy, and he had advised that the girl was in jail. The girl had advised her supervisor that there was an altercation between them—not on our premises—and that she had been arrested and had a one hundred foot restraining order against him. As an employer, I could not ensure that she would always be a minimum of 101 feet away. Our plant is sizable but we do have common areas like the break room and the parking lot. I felt awful but decided to let her go, as I had to hold up the law. The unemployment judge disagreed and granted her unemployment. Now, I do realize that unemployment security is not about me as a company and whether I did anything wrong but more about the situation and if the person should be able to collect unemployment. However, I have to pay into unemployment if I lose any cases.

That is another really nice fact about a business-friendly state. The taxable wage base *decreased* to $7,000 in 2023 (from $10,000 in 2022). Unemployment tax rates for experienced employers in the 2023 tax year will range from 0.07 percent to 18.78 percent (0.08 percent to 20.93 percent in 2022). The new employer rate will remain at 2.0 percent. In

Illinois, an employer's Benefit Ratio of 1.5299 percent is multiplied by the 2023 State Experience Factor of 127 percent to get 1.9430 percent, which rounds to 1.9 percent. After adding the Fund Building Rate of 0.55 percent, the employer's 2023 contribution rate is determined to be 2.45 percent!

Chapter 8
How to Hire/Recruit a New Workforce

Hiring people is an art, not a science, and resumes can't tell you whether someone will fit into a company's culture.

—Howard Schulz

Recruiting

The regional and state level workforce development was both a huge help and also a huge disservice. As previously explained, they did not have a good understanding of what was actually happening within the community from a workforce perspective. My bad. Their strategy made sense to me, so I gave it the credence it deserved. However, like me, they did not understand the "family" or "trust" phenomenon either. Why would they? It is not their world. Further, the mindset of a laborer versus a college educated person is vastly different. The answer here is to get the local workforce development people involved in helping you with strategic hiring.

In my first few months of moving here in 2019, I was floored when an employee told one of my leads that I need to prove myself. *What?* We are paying you more than you have ever been paid. We are offering more benefits than any other employer in the community, and we need to prove ourselves? Yes, back to family and trust. What the employee was really saying was: I don't know you. I don't trust you. Therefore, why should I do anything for you, like work, even though you are paying me?

First, you must decide how you will become the employer of choice. Integrating yourself into the community is step one. Step two is deciding how you will set yourself apart from other employers. How? Wages and benefits are where it is at. You will need to decide what wage you will start people at regardless of skill set. Remember, if you decide to use government programs, the government has a fundamentally union mindset. Everyone gets paid the same.

Interview other employers in the community. What are they paying on average? This should help you come to a conclusion. Also, what is minimum wage for the state you are moving to? In my case, minimum wage is $7.25 per hour, which is insanely low in my opinion. However, Mississippi also is one of the lowest cost of living states as well. I essentially have three departments performing very different functions. I came out of the gate saying that I would hire any CNC operator trainee at $13 per hour. I would hire anyone for the assembly department at $11/hour, and anyone in the heading department would be at $15 per hour. Cold heading is definitely skilled labor, and it is the hardest job in the plant, especially when your job is not running well. These wages were decided upon in June of 2019, before COVID. More than likely, it would be different today.

We single handedly raised the pay rates for many of the other local manufacturer's. This was not intentional, just a byproduct of our situation. But the community as a whole benefited. Many were only paying $8 to $10 per hour. Many people were leaving their current work because they trusted my general—and I was paying substantially more.

Chapter 8

Benefits? Coming from Illinois, our benefits were already good, and in comparison to local employers, fucking fantastic. I offer health, dental, and vision. You more than likely will have to change providers depending on the state and area you move to. Dental and vision are add ons at the employee's expense. In retrospect, though I have not changed the plan, I would find out what most people need. I have many peeps turning down health but taking dental. Dental is a big deal in my community. Remember, benefits need to benefit your team.

Paid time off. For clarification, we only offer paid time off. We do not do vacation and sick days. To me, this simply establishes a lying situation between you and your employee. Time off is time off in my book, and it is none of my business why you want to take the time. However, if someone is out more than three days without prior notice, I do require a doctor's note to return to work so that I know that they are okay to actually work. In Illinois 2024, you will no longer be able to request any documentation of any kind for people who miss work. I personally just think it is good business practice to request documentation, as many don't take care of themselves. Further, from a legal aspect, the employer may be held liable for a health concern that they don't even know about as the employee is not required to share it. To me, it is like enforcing safety glasses. I seem to care more about my employees' safety than they do.

Our old policy was to start accruing PTO time after ninety days. Further, the first year was forty hours of PTO. Our new policy allows accrual day one and first year of PTO as eighty hours. I also allow people to be extended twenty hours of paid time off, even if they have not yet accrued it.

In addition, we have eight to nine—depending on the calendar year—days of paid holidays. We used to have a waiting period of ninety days to be eligible, but that is no longer the case. I also, previously and have continued to pay the temporary labor the holiday as well. Treat people the way you would want to be treated. Yes, of course I lose and labor walks, etc. But I also win, as I believe people recognize that I did not have to pay them and appreciate it.

That is what I did to become the employer of choice. Subsequently, I also incorporate random pizza days, hotdog days, chili days, candy surprises, and annual winter and summer events. Food down here is how you show your appreciation. Food is a sign of family and bonding. I usually bring food to meetings, as it helps the meetings go along better, but it has taken on a new life force all its own.

Job Descriptions

Workforce development will advertise and hold a job fair for you. *This is great.* They will want you to have jobs available with detailed descriptions and in what pay category. They will also want you to have a path of career advancement laid out. Honestly, I don't think this work paid off, but again, I am being told what to do by a government agency, so one needs to oblige. I guess my point is that I exerted quite a bit of energy in putting it all together, and I don't think I got any real results from my efforts. Regardless, you do what you have to do.

Every community has ACT workforce keys testing. From ACT. org, ACT® WorkKeys® assessments are the cornerstone of the ACT workforce solutions. The assessments help you measure the workplace skills that can affect your job performance. WorkKeys assessments are:

- **Unique**—Unlike other assessments, they don't simply give an indication of reading and writing competency. Instead, they measure a range of hard and soft skills relevant to any occupation, at any level, and across industries.

- **Recognized**—Successful completion of WorkKeys assessments can lead to earning an National Career Readiness Certificate® (NCRC®)—a credential that verifies foundational workplace skills. Tens of thousands of employers recognize the value of the NCRC, and many recommend the credential to candidates.

With WorkKeys, you're in control. You can take the assessments on your own time, as many times as you want, and only share scores with employers when you're ready. Each assessment offers varying levels of difficulty. The levels build on each other, incorporating the skills assessed at the previous levels. For example, at Level 5, individuals need the skills from Levels 3, 4, and 5. The complexity can also increase as the quantity and/or density of the information increases.

Initially, I based my hiring off of these assessments. I would not recommend it. Why? I hired platinum, silver, and then bronze. Most of the applicants were at bronze level. Bronze level is basic. People can perform simple math and literacy questions. These tests do not necessarily show one's potential to learn. These tests do not indicate the blood pressure or anxiety level of the test taker, potentially lowering their score simply due to stress. These tests do not show one's motivation or initiative.

For the most part, having folks go and take the test is really a waste of time. It slows down the pace of hiring, as tests are only administered on certain days of the week, and then it takes time for the results to come back. At the end of the day, as employers hiring unskilled labor, you need the willingness to learn and the ability to show up. However, there is a "mechanical" test that while the people who took it did not do well, we discovered that if they scored anything, we were ahead of the game. So anyone we interviewed who was thought to have potential in the heading department was asked to take this test. But I still did not have the application knowledge to discern who to hire.

I did have everyone fill out a job application. In retrospect, this is the only tool I would use. I would use a standard short form application of job history. I would ask for highschooler graduation or GED, and I would ask what they do in their spare time. Hobbies in my opinion are far more telling of people's capabilities than previous jobs. Depending on the community, you can call previous jobs to confirm employment, but most do not respond to those calls here. I was a bit aghast, as that is rude. Where I am from, it is a requirement to validate someone's previous employment. Not here.

I have become an expert at reading employment applications. I have determined that generally speaking, applicants fit into four categories. First are people who take their job seriously. They are reliable. They want to come to work, do their job, get paid, and go home. This is your ideal applicant. Hire them and ask them if they have any friends who would be interested in employment, as often they have friends with similar values. However, they will not refer anyone until you have developed the know, like, and trust factor. I have an internal referral program, but it is seldom used. I have discovered that people do not wish to put their reputation on the line for someone else.

Category two is the "working the system" category. If the application shows three jobs held for four to six months with a year between each job, they are working the system. Depending on your state, the length of unemployment varies. Mississippi unemployment can pay for a year. With this employee, depending on where you are in your job hiring, they will be a good employee until month five or six. At months five or six, they start having attendance issues so that you can fire them, and then they can go collect unemployment again. Most employers do not challenge unemployment, which I find interesting. I have done my fair share of stopping this cycle, as I am the chargeable employer and fight every unemployment claim, and I have rock solid records.

My point is that this is an employee that is hireable, trainable, and will be agreeable and easy to work with until month five or six. In the beginning, yes, hire them. Just know to hire their replacement in four months. A painful way to manage your workforce, as we all know how expensive training can be. But until you develop that know, like, and trust in your community, you really have no other choice. Even now, this is not a bad strategy if you have a short-term influx of work. These folks can be hired to do unskilled jobs, allowing your core team to move to more difficult tasks for the short term and then move them back.

Category three is the "unemployable" category. If the application has repeated jobs at less than three months longevity, you are dealing with the chronically unemployed. These people want a job. They do not know how to keep a job. You do not have the ability in a restart or a startup to manage these folks. After being here for three years, I am finally able to start addressing the problem for which I was hired to solve originally.

Yes, what the community originally wanted from me was to get the unemployable working and being productive citizens of society. It was framed up as we have good hard working people who need jobs—but we have no industry.

Category four are second-chance employees. They are another great avenue. This is not on your job application, but often uncovered in an interview. They have to leave work every week or every other week to meet with their parole officer or get a drug test. Some companies are adamant about not hiring these folks. I am adamant about hiring them. They tend to be great employees unless they are actively using. The only second chance that I do not hire is violent crimes. I simply do not want to expose that to my workforce. Now being in Clarksdale, the majority of my team has served time at one point or another.

I was hiring through the state program, and two of the folks were arrested for fraud in the time frame of filling out their application with me and the government agency. The lady that I always work with at the agency called to let me know. I already had been made aware, and I said, "Obviously I cannot hire them, as they are in jail. I have no issue in hiring second chances, but they have to be out of jail!" Her response was, "Oh, we all know you have no issue with second-chance employees—most of your people." I laughed and thought it was good. I do not have an issue with being an example of things working.

I am also putting the over fifty-eight years of age in this category. Many employers do not wish to hire a short term, more expensive employee. My thought is why not? They are not going to job hop. It is out in the open that they are only going to work for a shorter period of time. They come with the needed experience and knowledge, making them easy to train. The best part is that you have time to find, recruit, and train their replacement.

Job Fair

Workforce development did an amazing job at our fair. We had 264 people show up. I only brought myself, my plant manager, and production supervisor. We could in no way talk with each of these people individually in an eight hour day. I don't think that they thought so many people would turn out either. The fair started at 8:00 a.m. I showed up at 7:30 a.m., and there was a line around the civic center. Crazy.

Again, I was advised to go off ACT work keys testing as a method to cut people. Today, I would have each person fill out an application. Longevity wins. They get interviews. The rest, interview for people who might have transferable job skills. I always ask what their hobbies are. Hobbies are very telling. Anyone who rebuilds engines, works on cars, bikes, etc. gets hired. Interview those who appear to be on the straight and narrow path.

They did tell me that there would hopefully be 200 applicants. I didn't believe them. If I were to do it again, I would have brought four folks along to interview people and the general and HR person would be there too, if you were successful in hiring those positions. Also, a key component in conversations is the question of whether they will come to you for training. If that answer is no, then your answer has to be no or not now as well.

I hired at this point. I would not do that again. I would take—if available—150 of the applicants and come back for one-on-one interviews. Due note, we spoke with some great people who were already employed. Not one of them came over. We were new. I did not know about community integration and getting people to warm up to us. We were an unknown entity and had not built a know, like, and trust factor yet. Working on it, but it had not yet happened. People do not like change, as change is risky. Further, people don't know if you will last.

I found out after eighteen months that there were actually bets being placed on whether or not we would survive, by prominent members in the community no less. I also found out that only one person had bet on us. His comment was, "Hell yes, they are going to make it." They both moved here. This is investment.

Hiring

If you are in an area that has high unemployment or high poverty, you will get solid applicants that are currently employed and simply fishing. While I wholeheartedly believe that you should do what you can to recruit them, keep in mind that people do not like change, and even if they are in a job that they hate for whatever reason, the known is better than the unknown. Moving to a new community, you are an unknown. It does not matter how long you have been in business. That, my friend, is irrelevant.

The other applicants are going to be in the other categories previously discussed, working the system, don't know how to hold a job, or second chance. Since the poverty rate was so high, and I did not know what I know now, I had a bitch of a time in hiring. I could hire all day long, but what I did not realize is that I was hiring eager folks who did not know how to work.

I knew I was in trouble when each of these folks showed up late on day three, and when it was discussed, they said, "You mean I have to show up *every day* at 6:00 a.m.?" in utter disbelief. I finally figured out the ratio of hiring to retention was literally 8:2. Hire eight, retain two. Often, those two were people who were working the system. Again, not that I agree with that life strategy. Had I known, I would have completely rethought the process.

What I did was hire in cohorts. I hired as many people as the current team could manage in disruption. For us, this was eight, and I also fully learned that within one month, I would be down to two. The volume of hires also depends on training and the criteria set forth by the workforce development college. They paid for training, but I had to have five people show up for each session. Again, I did not realize the challenge in what I was managing, so initially, I only recruited five into a cohort, and when one did not show up, I was spoken to very sternly about the rules of the road.

Chapter 9
How to Train a New Workforce

The only thing worse than training your employees and having them leave is not training them and having them stay.

—Henry Ford

Initial Training

How does training work best for you? What does your training look like? Is it a long or short cycle? Whatever it is, double it. Our training cycle for basic CNC operators with no setups, no touch ups, simply loading and unloading pallets, pushing start, and basic quality control checks was two weeks. We now allow four weeks.

How are your processes? Do you have rock solid processes in place? If you answer yes to this, I would challenge you to rethink that answer and test it. We started looking at moving two years before we made that decision. In those two years, I really focused on working on process templates. Developing them where none existed, as well as reviewing and updating existing process directions. I thought mine were solid. I was so wrong.

Whether you move or not, my advice is to get these processes in place. Our veteraned workforce and tribal knowledge is going away. The younger generations are not staying with companies for lengths of time. They are working for several years and then making a job change. The higher turnover rate is inconvenient but manageable. However, the hundredth monkey effect will not be as strongly in play as it once was.

The hundredth monkey effect is the result of a study done back in 1952 on a Japanese island where a scientist followed and documented the behavior of a single monkey. One day, the monkey washed its potato in the water before consuming it. The rest of its relatives started doing the same, then its friends. When the hundredth monkey followed suit, the behavior reached critical mass, and then all the monkeys on the island washed their potatoes immediately. This energetic transfer of knowledge was dubbed the hundredth monkey effect.

My new process in testing procedures is to have someone who has never done the job before see if they can do it. I don't mean someone else in the same department, but someone from a different department, not excluding admin. If they can do it without questions, you are probably good to go. Not always, though, as it depends on the confidence of the trainee. My newest approach is to make a video of the process and post it on our private YouTube channel so people can have a live reference. People learn in different modalities—visual, audio, kinesthetic, etc. Remember, a new workforce, even if your pay and benefits are good to great, is not necessarily an engaged workforce. Training requires engagement, and if you don't have the tools out the gate, then the likelihood of success is minimized.

I will be addressing the pace of move in the next chapter, but we have to touch on it here as it is a big consideration. I was advised by consultants to move as quickly as possible. That is not bad advice, as it is inherently expensive to keep two facilities in play. I would advise you to figure out how long you can keep two facilities running and structure the move and training around that timeline.

If your current workforce will travel to train, I would suggest you move the equipment first and do the training at the new location. The reason being is that most of the trainees initially hired had never been out of Clarksdale. Learning a new job in a new location is stressful. This does not give you a clear indication of the people who have been hired. People are better behaved when they are uncomfortable. We brought the CNC team in for two weeks for training. This was not a complete failure—but it almost was. When we sent them back to Clarksdale and moved the equipment over the weekend, it was as if no training had occurred at all. Then we had attendance issues.

If I could do it again, I would hire people and put them into a month of essential skills training. Yes, a month at least. This will immediately weed out the people who don't know how to work. Set the hours the same as the plant. Ours would be 6:00 a.m. to 2:30 p.m., if you can get the workforce development college to do that for you. That is a tall order. Review the essential skills training syllabus and modify it to make it more representative of what you need. For instance, the canned class from Clarksdale has computer training in their class. Our operators do not need computer training. Yours might. Essential skills also covers the importance of attendance, being on time, dressing appropriately, respect, consideration for others, and more. If you are in an area where you need to do essential skills training, then assume all of these "basics" need to be taught. If they cannot follow through in this training, then you can start re-recruiting before you even move the department. The college bought us Fanuc control boards. Basic training on these would also be part of essential skills.

Further advantages of investing your training dollars into essential skills is that the teacher can give you valuable insight into the recruits. They will indeed be able to tell you who will succeed and who won't. The teacher will also be able to advise you of short-term versus long-term employment expectations. The workforce development college designed an essential skills class. It was four hours a day, four days a week for two weeks. I did this route per other outsiders' suggestions, and it did not pay off. Again, the college is not in the midst of our reality. I was ignorant in thinking that they knew their workforce. They do know their workforce when you speak to the officials in general, but this doesn't translate into decisions around the reality of workforce development.

Get the equipment moved and have the home team go to the new location and spend time training there. Again, double the amount of time. In order to not burn out your current workforce, I would move in phases by department so it looks like a rotational move versus a department move.

Focus on the basics in training and developing a workforce. I learned some hard lessons but not doing this. In order to keep production pace, we actually had trainees changing tooling and doing touch offs in our CNC department. Looking back, that was bat shit crazy. Our tooling bill the first year was close to $100,000. The normal budget is $40,000. Our down time was insane due to all the crashes, and our scrap rate was off the charts. I believe our first year of scrap in the CNC department was somewhere in the neighborhood of $250,000 versus our regular rate of $20,000 annually. Those are some big numbers.

Basics only, people. Yes, you will have some people with innate talent who just "get it." But mostly that is not what happens. We need to keep in mind that depending on the area you move to, people may have not ever worked in a manufacturing facility until now. It is not the same as flipping burgers at McDonalds. The only transferable skill is showing up on time.

Chapter 10
Pace and Logistics of the Move

Speed is the greatest weapon in the battle against time.

—Dick Taylor

Announcement

The economic development group will want to announce or do a press release before the ink dries on that contract. Of course, it is a coo for them—especially the more down trodden the town. We signed in June, and we negotiated three weeks for the press release, which was not very long. We wanted to tell our employees and get feedback first. In today's world, you cannot risk your team members finding out about a major corporate decision via social media or the news. I have been shocked about what people have been able to find out about me. Google your name some time and see what comes up—you might be surprised.

Pace of Move

I touched on this a bit in the training section. The pace of the move obviously needs to be strategically laid out. We started our move at the end of July and completed the move in November 2019. We had a 67,500 square foot facility with a four door enclosed dock, and two docks were being used to hold inventory. In other words, we were pretty solidly packed. Moving that sized facility in four months and doing our best to maintain production was fast. We moved one department at a time. This was easier to manage, but in hindsight, I don't think it was in our best interest to move it in this fashion.

I would suggest—while it may be more costly—to move what you can manage to get up and running in the new location while continuing to produce in the old location. In other words, we did a mass move. I would not do that. I would move like three pieces at a time, get them up and running in the new location. I would pull the targeted folks for each piece of equipment out of essential skills training to assist with incoming equipment.

One of our challenges was that we had these people hired, and they came here for training, so how do we keep them engaged while we move? My hindsight plan covers all this and hopefully reduces employee turnover and scrap. But you don't know what you don't know.

Strategy

In any massive change up, you need to have a strategy behind how you will accomplish the task. In a massive move, you need to have a front end and a back end. Who will go and prep the new facility? The facility we moved into had been vacant for five years. While not an incredibly long time, certainly long enough for some deterioration to happen. The county did have funding for us to rehabilitate parts of the facility, but it still needed to be overseen. The place was filthy—normal for a long-term vacancy. My brother and I decided that he would do the front end and I would take care of the back end. Three of our employees who were moving with us went with him in July 2019.

Part of our strategy was to buy a house in Clarksdale. A place where we could land. I lovingly call it the "group" home. He and two others moved in while they looked for permanent housing. This was a very good decision. Though odd in that here I am in my mid-fifties moving, back in with my brother and living with various team members. Even more odd is that it worked really well. Who would have thought?

The time between signing and moving required lots of trips to Clarksdale. Gratefully, our quality manager had his graduate degree in industrial engineering and he was able to do a floor plan. If you do not have an industrial engineer on staff, I would highly recommend outsourcing for this very purpose. Another option is to call a local college and see if they have internship possibilities for their students, and better yet, if they have any grants for employers who are able to accommodate an internship.

We started moving the CNC department in August 2019 after training. We had several team leads who were not going to move with us but would help with the move. We loaded the trucks on Friday, and they left on Friday to meet the equipment on Saturday. Wired it up, and we were rolling on Monday. It is amazing what can happen when you have it lined out.

Logistics

How do you plan on moving the rest of the plant? This is the tricky part, believe it or not. We have tooling coming out of our ears. You know the one time job that just might come back. This is a time to purge, and even with purging, you will still have a shit ton to pack and move.

The obvious answer is to move via full truck loads. Go into your shop and advise me how many full truck loads you need. Yes, some guess work is required. I guessed thirty full trucks were required, and I used twenty-eight. If you have a logistics person, which was me, they should be able to put you in the ballpark. Further, someone needs to negotiate freight rates, in writing, for each move. In that negotiation, include how many hours you have for notice. Meaning, how much time does the chosen company need to get you a truck. Until the very end of the move, you will only be moving one or maybe two trucks a week or every other week.

I was not as well versed in logistics as I am now. Because of a combination of COVID and the move, I have become very familiar with logistics, but that is now. Previously, I did not have a good handle on how trucking companies operate. Most trucking companies cannot manage this requirement. They are a bit like construction companies. "I need this today." "I can get you one truck tomorrow." They are more, for lack of better words, fly by the seat of your pants. I could tell them in advance what I needed, but they could not deliver. I started with Schneider, and the first two bills came in as quoted by my sales representative. The subsequent bills were substantially more, and then we had accounting issues. My sales representative quit or was fired, and they could not schedule. It was a bit of a mess.

I then went to a brokerage service, CH Robinson. Who did a much better job in getting me trucks lined up, but the trucks tended to fail in showing up. This is not on them but on the brokered truck companies.

Knowing what I now know, I would go with a smaller brokered service that specializes in full truck loads. The reality is that even if they have their own trucks, they still broker out. Schneider was too large of a corporation. You need a mid-size, still large, but mid-size in comparison company that actually is more engaged in getting your freight done. Because of my recent experience, I could direct you to several different companies that would manage this much better than what I had to deal with.

Freight changes daily. Therefore, companies are extraordinarily reluctant to price thirty trucks over a three month period. Get your three favored, and get them quoting against each other. For the most part, you have time to wait until the end of the move when you are down to only a few employees. There is the mid-cycle crunch where you have no space in your plant and need to get it out.

How do you decide what goes when or what goes on what truck? Tape the dimensions of a fifty-three foot trailer out on your floor. Pack there. Heavier items toward the front. You have to be careful with weight. A full truck load is 44,000# max. We have a lot of heavy material, so I put trucks together with just material and trucks together with material and tooling or shop supplies. Depending on what you are moving, it needs to be packed appropriately.

At that point in time, we had 4,400# of coils that were not on a pallet, not on a carrier, and needed to be strapped in using two by fours to prevent them from sliding. Your shipping department needs to know how to do this. They may not. They may just be the recipients of these deliveries. If you need assistance, your supplier's logistics department can help.

Packing takes forever. If you have moved your home, you know how much time and work packing consumes. I am telling you straight up, your team will not be able to manage it. Further, it becomes more difficult when you start sending team members out to train. Hire temporary workers. We are talking about packing which does not require a critical skill set. If they don't show, get another one in. Take the pressure off your team.

Structure

Another part of your strategic plan needs to be the structure of the move with your raw and finished goods. This is pretty innate. However, I am going to spell it out, as the shipping end was solid, and my receiving end was not. It would have been helpful if my shipping and receiving person would have gone to Clarksdale to meet the freight, but he refused. Yes, he was one of the employees who called to see if we were still in business.

The day after the equipment moves, send the raw materials required for that equipment based on jobs you need to run. Send tooling as well. This is how the move needs to be done.

Determine if you plan on continuing to ship finished goods out of the old location or the new location. We continued to ship finished goods out of the old location. Prior to the move and before the announcement of the move, do a full physical inventory count with bin locations.

I had the shipping department write the bin location on the box. This way when the racking was disassembled and moved we could put it all right back where it was supposed to be. My ERP was updated, as well as the racks and labeled boxes. I seriously thought this was the least of the challenges. Wrong. I was still in Illinois and really should have gone to Mississippi to meet the inventory and manage that. My new shipping person was not experienced enough in this type of activity to take the lead. I have to accept responsibility for my failure in leadership.

What happened is that my two youngest team leads took charge—and no, they did not call to run it by me. They put up the racks not in the order in which they were shipped. The racks were banded and labeled when they left. Upon unpacking, they were not reassembled in the same bundle. This would have been fine, as all the racks were labeled. But when they loaded the palleted finished goods, they just threw them on any racking.

Years ago, prior to having a more formal approach to inventory management, we at least had inventory on the shelf based on type and size of product. Still hard to find, but at least you knew you were in the ballpark. The finished goods was completely fucked. The part that should have been the easiest was a nightmare.

I did not realize this happened until I physically moved in November 2019. I could not figure out why we were not keeping up in shipping. They literally could not find the product. We were so far behind in shipping that by the time I got there, it felt hopeless. Customers were irate, and I was a complete bitch. I knew we had the product, but could not find it. In overwhelm, it is interesting to review the poor decisions your oxygen-suffering brain makes. Instead of just not shipping and removing all the inventory, we just suffered through it. On the weekends, I would go in and rearrange inventory to at least get it by type. Again, the boxes were labeled. The racks were labeled. It was all in our ERP, yet we just continued to struggle.

Remnants

While you now have the tools, supplies, equipment, and raw materials out and your shop is empty, you still have work to do. Gas and propane tanks need to be picked up. Oil bins need to be removed. If you own your facility and plan on renting it out or selling it, it needs to be cleaned up. My cold heading department is oily. After the heading equipment moved, there was a mess. It is interesting to note that people are not necessarily very helpful when it comes time to close contracts and services.

Uniforms are one of those things that are difficult to close out. Collecting all your employees' uniforms is a process, and settling up is another process. Rags , another pain point: *do not get me started*. Regardless, it all needs to be settled out and agreed upon.

Getting the tanks and drums and the rest of the items that needed to get out was not easy. Suppliers said they would come and pick it up, and they didn't. It got to the point where the only thing left was to go to a building and sit on the floor in the office and wait for people to show up. This was unfriendly, as I also had to keep my eye out due to the fact that the internet did not function in the warehouse because of the metal roof. Gratefully, one of our previous employees agreed to go and meet people for final pick up of such remaining items.

Chapter 11
Aftermath

Grit is having the courage to push through, no matter what the obstacles are, because it is worth it.
—Chris Morris

Women

(Guys, you will get something from this too.)

I didn't get there by wishing for it or hoping for it, but by working for it.
—Estee Lauder

The move was huge, and is still a huge culture shock to me. I still often suffer from—oh, right, we are not in the north any longer syndrome. Oddly, the thing that I hate the most is the thing I love the most. When I first moved, I would ask someone to do something, and they would say sure, in a minute. Days would go by, and I would ask again. A minute in the south is not a literal minute, ever. A minute in the south could be within the hour, or it could be days. I call it a southern minute and a northern minute to help my team understand what my need is for that request.

On the other hand, if I am in a bind, the southern culture is to help. Up north, if I was in an emergency situation and called people to help me, it would be okay, I can get there in three hours. People are very willing, but just not able. Here, if I am in a bind, the response is I got you; be there in ten.

I also need to advise other women leaders that while you spend your life creating your reputation and expertise in your field, which commands respect among other industry leaders, do not for one second think that this transfers. Sadly it does not, especially in the south. For the first time ever, I am grateful to have a partner who has a penis. I went through all those presentations, and the southern men really were not speaking to me. You know what I mean. The sort of included me because on some level they knew that they needed to do that.

I cannot tell you how often I am in a meeting with my brother and an accountant, attorney, banker, etc., and I am completely disregarded. At a conference table, a man has his back turned toward me while he speaks directly to the rest of the penis owner players in the room. It is maddening. I am 50 percent of the equation, and without my "yes," it doesn't happen.

I used to talk with my brother about this up north, and it was not this blatant. It happens for sure but not that egregiously. I talk to him about it down here after every meeting, and actually, this is good for him. He now has been enlightened to the way that a female is treated. He now says, "I know; I see it. I don't know what to say about it."

Should I address it? I often ask this question. Up north, hands down, yes. Here, with all the changes we have made, I say pick your battles. I have decided that my end game is to win and succeed, and I need "x" to happen. Perhaps some ladies out there will think this is weak of me, and that is okay, as I sometimes think this is weak of me as well. However, I also think it is the stronger leader who does what has to get done, even if that means tolerating poor and tasteless behavior.

I have been here for three years now and really felt that I needed to communicate my experience. I have learned a lot about human nature, culture, community, and myself, and I have had more personal growth than I intended or consciously wanted. We risked it all and betted on ourselves. We uprooted a forty-three-year-old company and shortly after our move had to deal with a world pandemic. I wish I had had the information that I have now then. I am all for innovation and improvement. We certainly have upleveled the company. I do think that while my workforce is two years old and less, we are actually a stronger company than we were before we moved.

It never occurred to me that I would not have the outside resources available to me that I took for granted. As a result, we have become almost 100 percent self-sufficient. We used to send *all* of our products for outside processing, cleaning, passivating, annealing, brazing, etc. Due to freight and time delay issues, which became a huge problem with COVID and still remains a problem, we had to invest in equipment to bring those operations in-house. We now clean and passivate all our products in-house. We found equipment that wasn't perfectly sized but does the job at a one and a half year ROI, which is amazing.

Our brazed parts, which we needed turned immediately, were a complete train wreck with the supplier. Sadly, due to transit issues, our supplier was completely frustrated with how the product was showing up—damaged—and they blamed us. They wanted us to hotshot, expedited freight, every load. Financially, that was just not feasible. I did consider buying a sprinter truck and hiring a driver to drive to Illinois on Monday. Wait for the product and drive back on Friday, but that is high risk. We looked at brazing lines in Illinois, and brazing lines need a lot of room, which we did not have, not to mention the cost of a custom line. Even not investing in a custom line was crazy expensive. What used to be a one-week process started becoming two or three, and that is if the freight showed up. We had so many lost pallets and more damaged with parts missing. This was killing my on-time delivery with my accounts.

Miraculously, a lead came over eBay for some brazing equipment. It was picked up at an auction, and the guy wanted to sell it. It was exactly what we needed. He had it listed for $20,000. He either did not know what he had or just needed to dump it. We offered him $10,000, and he took it. Normally, we are talking about $250,000 at least.

But we did not know how to braze, and coming up to speed on that was an expensive education. However, it solved our delivery issues. Our parts look *far* better than the work our supplier did. Our fall out is much less than the fallout from the supplier. Found out that if you have fall out you can re-braze. Our supplier for *years* told us that we couldn't run parts through again. I don't necessarily know that I am saving money from when we were in Illinois—I think I am, but due to having to add labor and the cost of maintenance, it might be a break-even situation financially. However, quality and on-time delivery win every time.

The other somewhat sad and disturbing thing I learned about in this move is that friends are really a reason, season, or lifetime. Interestingly enough, my best friend forever completely dropped me as a friend. I was extraordinarily hurt but after two years have come to terms that my friendship was one of need. On the other hand, people that were initially acquaintances when I moved have become amazing friends. Further, I have made some amazing friends in my new town. It takes a long time to build a village and admittedly I took my village for granted.

I am in the midst of rebuilding and am so grateful every day for the people I can count on, and am so excited when I meet new friends.

I have only had one person from industry ask me if I am glad I moved. A year into it, the answer was definitely no. Two years, definitely no. Three years, yes. Especially now that Illinois has decided to further its reach into private business with its new labor laws going into effect in 2024. I still have to deal with it, as I have employees left in that state, but only a handful. Statistically, a new business takes five years of traction to be a sure thing. A restart business takes two years to determine its survival. Gratefully, we survived. I survived.

Had I known the information given in this book, my life would have been so much different. Hindsight is twenty twenty, as they say, and once again, this has been proven.

Possibility

I hope that this book has given you some insight into what is possible and to open your mind to other options. I know so many people who feel stuck in their current location. You are not stuck; only in your mind are you really stuck. Entrepreneurs are typically all about risk and stepping out of the box. We all have thought leadership, and we move forward by taking action because entrepreneurship is fucking hard.

I did not write this book to imply that you are bad if you don't move. This book is intended to be a guide in moving if you choose. It is so that you don't make the same mistakes that I made, and for the life of me, I don't know why nobody talks about this. Maybe it is because I am a woman, and we naturally share and collaborate. I would not want anyone to risk their life's work and fail.

This book is also intended to encourage you to make your organization stronger through the lessons I learned from uprooting the business. Strategic process development. Strategic hiring. Strategic training. All these things that I learned can be applied to your existing business to make it that much better and more competitive.

Chapter 12

The common idea that success spoils people by making them vain, egotistic and self-complacent is erroneous; on the contrary it makes them, for the most part, humble, tolerant and kind.

—W. Somerset Maugham

Conclusion

My desire is that this book leaves you with hope. In determination, there is success. In risk, there is success. In failure, there is success. First, and most importantly, keep an open mind. You can do what you think you can do. If you don't think you can move twenty-five plus miles away for whatever reason—I can list a thousand excuses, as I have heard plenty—then you can't. What is your belief system about what is possible? About what you can accomplish? This is not simply about moving locations but really about any avenue in business and your life.

If you consider moving or opening a new division mileage away from home base, you ought to look at your motivation. What will this action give you? Things to think about are quality of life, labor availability, labor cost, cost of living, taxes, insurance, and workman's comp insurance.

What is the most important goal for you, and is it financial or personal?

Act as if you are going to move. You have mentally opened that door, so start thinking about the what-if. What has to be in line in order to make this happen? Making these shifts within your company will only strengthen it, regardless of actually moving. These actions should be taken anyway, it is just not urgent, so you don't do it.

Hire a move consultant to help you navigate and negotiate state and county grants. Determine how to narrow down the responses from economic development corporations. Remember an EDC would prefer to work with small businesses of fifty people and less. Smaller businesses are more likely to stay put and have a bigger impact on the community. Determine how you will vet the locations you choose to pursue.

All is on the table for negotiation from the building itself to payroll tax credits to moving expenses to training expenses. Remember the training expense needs to be a hefty budget. We had $300,000, and I would work toward $500,000 to $1 million.

You need to vet the workforce. Review the culture, the unemployment rate, the poverty rate, and the crime rate. All impact your workforce in one way or another. How committed is the workforce development college or programs to your lift? Are they truly your partner and will work with you regarding all the crazy needs that come up? What is the skill set of the community? What is taught in high school? What is taught in vocational schools? What other industries are in the community?

How will you manage your existing workforce? Can you negotiate with them to come train at your new location? What do they need to do that? What retention bonus will you give them? Will you help them get another job, and if so, how? To what extent? Have you beefed up production enough to manage the increased scrap rate from depressed employee morale? What will you do to entice your employees to make this move with you? Nothing is out of the question, including buying a house for your valued supervisor! This is a challenge for you to really think out of the box and to learn what your employees really need and want.

How will you recruit, train, and retain labor? If you have 30 percent of your folks moving with you—which is fabulous—you still need to figure out the remaining 70 percent. How can you set yourself apart and be attractive to viable prospective labor?

Finally, how will you strategically design the actual move from heavy equipment to your manufacturing supplies? How does the layout of your new facility look? Where will racking go? Consider the logistics of the move, not just the heavy equipment but all the raw materials, tooling, and manufacturing supplies. How will you organize the trucks? Where will you continue to ship products from? How will you transition from the old location to the new facility?

I sincerely hope I have inspired you to think a little differently about life and what is and what could be. I hope I opened your eyes to holding a different mindset about what is possible. You hold the keys, not your employees.

You want to learn more about what is possible?

Go to www.staciahobson.com or click on the QR code and grab your freebies.

Want more information? Go to my web page and click the work with me tab to connect. No worries, the tab does not sign you up for anything other than to ping me for more information.

You can also hire me to speak on moving but also all things manufacturing!

Let's connect! - I would love to connect with you on all social platforms.

You can find me on social @staciahobson

ACKNOWLEDGMENTS

I need to thank some awesome people for their support and efforts as this book would not be here if it wasn't for them.

My brother and business partner, Blake. If either one of us was a no on this decision, it would not have happened. We have been co-creating for a span of three decades with each creation larger than the last. It has been an exciting and sometimes terrifying journey, yet we somehow seem to land on our feet. My sister-in-law, Elizabeth. If she had said no to the move, this book would not have been written. Further, she was instrumental in the book cover design.

Thank you to the team members - Reddy, Travis, Mike - who believed in this move and supported it on so many levels and sacrificed so much. They hung in there even when it was unbelievably difficult. Cannot forget the Illinois employees who traveled back and forth or who just stayed in MS devoting numerous hours to get the company propped up, Ricardo, Joel, Eric, Sam and Don.

My friends who have listened to me countless times go on and on about all things book. The title, subtitle, cover design, back of the book, etc. You know who you are but just in case, Beth, Brian, Liz, Amanda, Rachel, Julia and Mike. Thank you for being there for me, encouraging & supporting me.

Thank you to Jake Kelfer, his team and his community that I lovingly call my bookies. This book would never have come to fruition without Jake's guidance and amazing coaching combined with the tough love from Joe VanGeison and of course everyone in the community..

Thank you to the city of Clarksdale MS as well as the state of Mississippi. Without the trust and support of Delta Strong, the move would not have happened. I owe huge thanks not only to Frank Howell, who closed and subsequently supported us by other means, but also Mitzi Woods, Workforce Director, as she stepped up when we needed it most. Lastly, Jon Levingston, EDC Director who worked diligently structuring the grants.and supporting our need for training. Then of course there were numerous community folks who supported this endeavor.

Thank you to our site selection consultants, The Next Move Group for negotiating phenomenal grant contracts.

Thank you to my editor, Shaina Clingempeel, team at miblart and my formatter Sophie Hanks. All of them contributed significantly to making this book a legitimate piece of work.

Finally, thank you to Steph, my father, who taught me what it means to have big balls.

About the Author

Stacia Hobson, co-owner of Image Industries Inc, began her career in the family business upon graduating college. Although her plan was never to work for the business let alone own it, she was the key driver in transforming the business from 100% distribution to 100% manufacturing.

Today, she runs operations for her family's multimillion-dollar manufacturing business serving nine distinct vertical markets. Learning to navigate the "family politics" provided a sturdy and durable foundation for future growth..

Stacia is acutely aware of what it takes to succeed as a woman in a male dominated, blue collar industry. She is passionate and proud to be in manufacturing as she feels that it is the backbone of the USA. With over three decades of experience under her belt, she has acquired extensive practical knowledge of business, relationships, and entrepreneurship.

Stacia is employing her vast experience to provide business consulting services to guide leaders of all sized businesses to embrace the bold decision-making needed to achieve massive transformation. Her expertise lies in unlocking new possibilities while helping clients navigate the risk associated with these courageous choices. She leads by example and leans on her experience as she herself has made many daring decisions. She aims to create a "ripple effect" by encouraging individuals and organizations to fearlessly pursue their ambitions. By instilling a sense of empowerment and self-belief, she encourages her clients to envision and achieve what were once perceived as brave goals.

Connect with Stacia on social at @staciahobson!

Made in the USA
Clarksdale, MS
01 November 2023

barcode of isbn

9 798989 304608

Made in the USA
Monee, IL
14 November 2023

46533600R00066